Vestige

I sincerely hope you'll enjoy my book,

With very best wishes

Anthony V Smith

Vestige

You're Not Alone

Royalties will go to

Cancer Research UK
Registration No. England and Wales 1089464
2 Redman Place London E20 1JQ

By Anthony Smith

Shoestring Book Publishing, Maine, USA

Vestige

Paperback & Hardcover are available

HardcoverVersion ISBN:
978-1-943974-33-7

Published by;

Shoestring Book Publishing

Maine, USA

Layout and design by Anthony Smith, and Shoestring Book Publishing. For information address;

Shoestring Book Publishing c/o Allan Emery
495 Penobscot Avenue
Millinocket Maine 04462

shoestringpublishing4u@gmail.com
www.shoestringbookpublishing.com

This Book is Dedicated to my brother Ray

Raymond John Smith, 18th Aug 1958 – 1st Aug 2020

I cried my eyes out the Saturday, after seeing by brother for the first time, bedridden. The bravery of many who are sadly on borrowed time, for Raymond, or, Ray to family, he had arranged his own funeral and a simple one that would not extend the grief for family and friends. It was to be a private affair to go it alone, like he had done for much of his life.

I personally was mortified and angry at first, but in my heart, I knew Ray, would not want to burden us any further. The worst moments are knowing there's not a lot one can do, other than be close. His transfer to the Villa Maria in South Croydon was eagerly awaited finally. Ray would be given the necessary 24hr care. It prevented me from breaking down completely, knowing he was now in capable hands. Before, Ray was having difficulty on lonely evenings and the early hours.

Unable to speak, it seems his silent stare had aroused us to participate in some way, to communicate, but not to exhaust him. "Constant talking", he once said, 'It tires me out', and so it was to reassure him. As I write, Ray's days are surrounded by care staff, and nurses who visit him often. At the Villa Maria care home, Ray would now be comforted. Of the siblings he was the only one who never married, and so, living alone meant his social life was going to be restricted. Sylvia, Patricia, and I would break away to find respective partners, but what of Ray I kept asking? His free spirit is something quite unique, and helping people was his trademark, being trustworthy and loyal, in help and friendship, and nothing seemed to worry him Ray was a brother who was innocently blessed, with a loving heart, it remains open, for us this day to remember him by.

To families and friends everywhere, it is when you read this book, it is hoped your waits for treatment and waiting time will seem shorter, plus all positive outcomes in the end will come your way.

Anthony Smith

A Personal Message

The practice of being neighbourly is very much a thing of the past. It is when you can separate your own way of life to spare a thought for someone's needs, then Ray in this case had three such neighbours who had assign themselves to him. For the lack of understanding today's society, the truth is, these three exceptionally kind and caring individuals, would become 'Good Samaritans' in their own right, coming to my brother's aid.

Take for instance…. Zarqa, [Zee], Ahmed
She found Ray at the steering wheel of his car, suffering from seizure. Her quick thinking got the ambulance within minutes, and to the hospital. Back home, her concerns were met with daily updates to us, and putting herself out being readily available. Ray would be bedridden, and dependent on Zee's passing and caring nature, until that was the Council's care was in place. For these kind acts we will be forever indebted.

Then, there is…. Frank Barrett
A neighbour who needed his own daughter, let alone helping others, but his help became saintly. That Ray now bedridden, his mind now unhurried was unable to love his dog 'Suzie' like he had done before. It was an exceptional ask for Frank to keep 'Suzie', but he did. While into care, Ray went and to the Villa Marie' care home, Frank would take the burden from Ray, and keep 'Suzie' for all time. I am sure Ray was mindfully aware and forever grateful to Frank for this beautiful deed.

"What can I say…? Peter Bint
There was a time when Ray would scuttle to the door, knowing his cancer was getting worse, to let me in. It was during this time, up until Ray's move to the care home Peter would become like a personal assistant, giving his help liberally, without fuss, carrying on regardless. While it is often shown St. Peter holding the keys of heaven, in reference to Peter Bint it cannot be argued he had done so much for Ray when it wasn't obligatory, yet he did what he had to do. Now this was an exceptional kindness in my books.

A Special Mention for the staff at St. Christopher's

Had it not been for the kind caring nurses of St. Christopher's Hospice who seemingly oversaw the care and attention my brother Raymond was receiving at home. Now, to pinpoint Mary who must have had 'alarm bells ringing', about my own confusion, then she must be singled out for praise for her beck and calls had kept me level-headed. In her absence my calls in vain put me in touch with nurses Joanna and Grace. Therefore, the beautiful way in which you've conducted yourselves, goes way over what is naturally a caring nature by what I've witnessed, it's rather unique, it must have come from so young an age.

It so happens for so sensitive a subject that you all seem to have said the right things, having heard from the offset, by one insensitive 'girl' from a hospital, [mention no names], who broke the news rather in a vain attempt to get off the phone.

I bring to your attention the St. Christopher's Hospice, Sydenham. It seems the concerns for my mental state were resolving matters progressively, one step at a time while feeling helpless and 'beyond help'. Having Mary, Joanna and Grace on call then I did not quite hit the buffers full on, thanks to them, and to think they do this kind of work each day, is truly remarkable, what you have done to raise my brother Ray's morale remains invaluable.

Praise also, for Grace who as part of the bereavement team at St. Christopher's Hospice. Her concerns came at the right time for me to call, it is to Grace, when thinking all was lost, it is thanks to her that I have now come to terms with Raymond's passing. It truly highlights St. Christopher's Hospice to praise not just those who have helped me personally, but to all the staff there. 2020 will stand out for good received, that one's trust can be brought to a whole new level by your calming influences.

Tony Smith

x

Mere words,
.... to exchange will substantiate long waits.
—*TITUS LLEWELLYN*

In aid of

CANCER
RESEARCH
UK

Contents

Foreword

The idea of a cobwebbed chair in the attic must have you wondering about the idea behind it. To think that many of us have had to come down from that attic, first, to face the truth. The response before making a fight of it, and making a stand for what good can come out of anything these days, even if the odds are stacked against us, fight anyway. To leave that chair, which long ago, many would have resigned themselves to, continues not to have us languish.

And yes, it is a highly sensitive subject, and so the wait. With treatments for cancer being favoured now, a lot of patience is needed still and so, having experienced 6 months wait for my mother and now my brother, 4 months, it tests our resolve with a range of emotions. Although Ray and I were very close, we could have been closer. For the way he led his life it was in many ways unchallenged. He would in the meantime, attend his chemotherapy appointments alone, and the waiting room with several old magazines we've read before, the sole purpose of the wait becomes clear.

And so, will the phoenix within you, rise..., impatience I can tell, can above all else be blamed for these anxiety levels, and with it, depression. Coping has very much to do with what we can do with this sit and wait. What this book clearly states is, we all have to, even if by flicking through the pages, then let this be the prerogative. But at some point, you will want to read, with possibly some palatable words to your liking. It's just like getting out that chair like many have done.

While at that lowest point, missing the woman I loved, poetry was literally forced upon me to write, by a work colleague who cared. And so, leaving that chair so to speak, to occupy my mind. Having found the perfect woman, I wasn't going to give up on distance. Maureen and I were married almost 29 years after initially finding each other. A totally different waiting room, granted, but discovering a new venture like writing, it got me through such a torrid time. And so, I shall ask you all to focus on the same, and keep busy, and share some quality time with those closest to you.

Anthony Smith

Preface

It is often in the field of poetics that 'Titus Llewellyn' is known in the U.S.A. To his family, it is Tony Smith, to poets around the globe, it is 'Sir', it is said, not as a title but as a mark of respect, to be approaching the end of a 'Full Poetical Works'. Sadly, Tony's brother was becoming more dependent on medical care. It was then the idea came about, to transfer some of those works for the good cause of Cancer Research UK. Of course, positive findings will provide and benefit the worldwide initiative to advance further research so we can eliminate Cancer someday.

To prevent the anarchy of the mind from taking over. It is in your best interests that certain reading material will therefore bring a result, you will probably wonder where all that waiting had gone. It is to benefit you all, that the 'allpoetry' website, [an American domain], would wish to adopt a fine British 'wine', the pleasure comes to uncork for you such a bottle, of 'Titus Llewellyn'. It is said, a man who can confine himself like he had done for many years, must surely bring from the vaults an exquisite taste, to serve all remnant, or trace. To conjure from this book, how great a feast, from beginning a worthwhile find. A year after the first date of publication, royalties are given by, Shoestring Book Publishing, to the author. From there, funds will be transferred to the Cancer Research UK Charity.

As a first, the works of Titus Llewellyn will be relatively new to the British public, therefore, we American's enjoyed an old world feel of what is to be expected. Our present-day poet has studied the Classics from as far back to 2500 years ago, it is sometimes textured along those timelines, a poet who we could have mistaken, coming from the 16th century to render his soul.

Charles Cuthbertson, [Florida, USA]

ACKNOWLEDGEMENTS

Maureen Smith, Wife and Confidante

Helping me through this difficult time, but for 3 exceptional neighbours, who did much of the work, thanks must go to my wife Maureen for supporting me throughout, whilst having Covid myself during an awkward time.

Peter Bint, Frank Barret, Zee Ahmed

To 'Love Thy Neighbour", referring to the Biblical, ethics of reciprocity cannot be more exaggerated than 3 exceptional neighbours, who became 'Good Samaritans' in their own right. They are singled out in, "A Personal Message

Sylvia, Dave and Jemma

To a sister, brother-in-law, and their daughter, for organising the removal of almost everything and being supportive to Ray in the later stages of his cancer and last days at the Villa Maria care home, South Croydon.

St. Christopher's Hospice, Sydenham

Nurse Mary for her visits to Ray and consoling me no end and nurses Joanna and Grace for their support on the phone lines, Grace from the bereavement team who helped wholeheartedly. [See, 'A Special mention'].

Villa Maria Care Home, South Croydon

Full appreciation to all care staff at 'Villa Maria', for their expertise in nursing and care. Not forgetting Debbie and Juliet both, who with a sympathetic ear, did a fantastic job for Raymond and our family.

To all Cancer Patients and their Families

My best wishes to all concerned for a positive outcome.

Vestige

People may smirk
      at poetry;
         but let me tell you,
    if we can leave behind
the physical side of ourselves
when all about us – those who cannot,
    I am more the man,
      than anyone before
        who didn't care,
  or didn't understand – then
flinch my friend some more,
    this vestige does.
        Amen.

Hortensia

The dew has hoisted in exalt as the sun arose
Umbels were yet to be seen, but bearing down,
Before we take to the stage, chlorophyll gown
Had gathered back its bold but beautiful pose.

Curtains I consider best while natures preen,
It gives bucolic scenes spring feeling, it shows
Unknowingly, the time and place high on toes,
Summer takes its place from a beautiful screen.

Lifting the auditorium sunlight, the superfluous
Adornment, tiny clusters adapt the many fractal,
Each to their own in modesty to become tactile
In unison and sway with a deep inner snugness.

I suggest the early summer, to initiate openings,
A 'Swan Lake', adventure, tinged with blue tips,
They'll dare not hesitate to wear the beige slips
Pure the ardent whispers birth of Venus brings.

It is together they will choose that one if it were
To keep fulfilment with this wonderful intimacy,
Ballerinas, who have instilled, innocent delicacy
Between themselves and the eye of the beholder.

For months on end, the flowering season, it will,
Entertain the audience the green fingered variety
Forever and a day will extend this social society
Free will, their petals are a supporting role decyl.

A French Garden

Distinctively there are dreams waiting in that chair,
What abundance my dear sweet-hearted hydrangea,
Balanced in a niche, with sheer romantic tales to air
Turning heads, they speak, among themselves here.

Pertaining to French exquisite styles, the larger hats
Are beautifully made, its kind stows more a façade
Forgetting where we are and we French bureaucrats
Of modest means most certainly use it as sunshade.

Overlooking privets have this unique vantage point;
Accept this as a clear understanding that we women
Shall be left alone, although for lady's nights anoint
A certain ambience, horizons hang its sacred omen.

It is well known that small be wonderful, the garden
Beyond the door, those dreams of ours who succeed
In such heat if seen to be lurking, I beg your pardon
As shade lovers, we must now worship a single need.

While the best of everything, such, the quaint places
We, the privileged few, we must appreciate this small
And evocative part of London a part of it embraces
It's somewhere private, somewhere that I do enthral.

The chair I recall, it separates our topic conversation
The scholar, who for reasons known to them, is fair
To share equally, the other plants, simply a donation
Part of a magnificent French connection to compare.

Not some city, I can well imagine, a wealth of luxury
A small realm East of where of far, the advantageous
Wise doctrine to think of small a place how motherly
Brumath occupies a site off the Roman Brocomagus?

Just one of many places, we the keepers of the secrets
Needless the wait, not to haste, though not to get lost
Many books I've read, are about my having no regrets,
Few friends, a life of wine my paradise, a prize riposte.

By Modest Means

In truth, by what you say Ernest Hemingway,
It links, - 'why should anybody be interested,
In some old man who was that failure?' I say,
Key to necessitate my own has been invested.

Failure in my rise, my fall may seem a corpse
But genuinely a friend, my mind's arboretum
Unknown glyphs, are likened to the Thorpe's...,
Tiny finds do conform in keeping a verbatim.

The Illusionary overlooks what is a jacquard
Merely architrave to finding out this rhetoric.
Theories will show them one's own backyard
My bougainvillea reasons within the esoteric.

Herringbone herein, it holds a stoic reminder,
It does prevail, the precious few who possess
Vast wealth of knowledge, more a pathfinder,
Too stubborn to novel over my latest success.

Constituents the many forms, as often, mood
Unfathomed depth which is asked of gypsum
To elaborate thought I find it quietly subdued,
The lamp of authority to carry-on its wisdom.

To substantiate ways in which I am portrayed,
Singularly this study of myself is now confined
Leopard print if fake I feel, my own shall fade,
Belonging to, it holds such a gentlemanly kind

The Perfect Storm

— Pelagic waves, satirical crusade, the mystery;
Lipase holistic frolics, multilateral
Physiques are wildly impressive, sheer blistery
Guffaw, a will to empower emollient collateral,
Orations, themes, create a percolative distillery
Confide in sate – abhor the derivative concern
Allegedly unabashed how moods stir to overturn.

Vast persuasions have gathered hostile,
Offshore, far from an anaphylactic qualm erstwhile
Achieves a height from heaven's nigh on seventh!

When perhaps, asking fate to collect the spill,
Enlightened by the minds of men the distinguished
Waves will be stubborn --- hopes will unfurl until.
It's written by the quill; Within this deluge
Emissary to Hermes who'll lift us… at times
Beyond the means one holds a conscious refuge
When beyond the means our conscious chimes
Pursue, at the rate of God knows, -- roll out the scrolls—
Higher still one climbs, is who controls?

When the ubiquitous Cronus, shall open wide, and swallow
Beguiling moments perfects the storm at heart
Maintaining lavish reprimand his children will, 'follow';
Calumnious outcomes the gryphon tears apart!

Unashamed the deaths that Phorcys could not save,
Serves as COURAGE— for each lost soul, a wave.

First Love, Like Still Waters

Where hardly a ripple is led to mention,
allow our reflections to react once stirred
that water has this lovely surface tension
evanescent to a glance if which preferred
reminds me of my first love apprehension.

Love's Exponential

astrorum communi

As far the distance and many light years,
Ours is nothing, yet love has travelled far,
Here under this umbrella, Capella appears
To bring me closer to you my nearest star.
Within this constellation whereby Auriga
Shines beyond the light, the angel chorus
Has kept the constellation home quadriga
To which adjacent souls placate to Horus.

Keeping a perusal while under your spell
This focus on you while the sky at night,
I thought might hold a secret, not to tell,
The reason why my love for you is right.

But for happenstance, for this upraising
The stars, for which this umbrella draws,
The constellation of Auriga it's amazing:
What love can find the vision it explores.

It is within our own space that we keep,
The secret of love with this night so vast
To keep our souls in, we will forage deep,
Within a means of making what will last.

Ode to Melancholy

Tho' woe begone I am found too deep,
my silent suffering has a credulous will
unwilling acceptance, it strives to keep
persistence edging towards that landfill.

5   Resentment of those the pain it carries,
such viciousness to move a past master
to exude fall and pain my twain it varies,
in all matters, relating to each disaster.

The difference is unhurried melancholy,
10   it has blatantly given us smaller mercies
which often forces us to choosing folly
to instigate the mind our outrage curses.

It leaves one as this indigenous species,
insurgence swore astutely, with a blithe
15   disgruntled sorrow as the will decreases,
bearing down, too wrought to be alive.

Yet grief defines how hoary overawed,
upon this discovery without it resolute
not far from keeping, my having stalled
20   much sleeping in this state of ill-repute.

The Arctic & the Walrus

You'll find northern most, battle weary weather,
Arctic ice, upon what the walrus said, to its child;
In walrus language, the microphone or whatever,
Sound would cup, 'Hey! Take her where it's mild'.

One Beautiful Time Piece

One beautiful time piece splendidly preserved,
A timeless possession that love 'twould outlast;
For a decade or more, with a parting observed,
And a love interaction that Folktale would cast

A mourning period holds an emptiness inside
And love has been held for as long as it takes,
Hopes keep the cogs moving, slowly to abide
Death, - my life has accounted many mistakes.

Indeed, as it was no one's concern I'll survive
Such is time to suspend this much of my faith,
For the good we put into it, love would revive
The blessing of God to keep us, and love safe.

O' beautiful time piece, seems this immaculacy
Which has distributed much ugliness elsewhere;
Beyond the lower reaches of banal, - compare
Distance from anywhere else, it ails inaccuracy?

Provenance was conceived it's now defamatory,
From what I have heard, this absurd fact of life
Slowing down the clock, that is found auditory
To movement, keeping with continuous strife.

That beauty is supine, with it being skin deep,
If something time can allow to have bestowed
Upon capture, I have incensed upon it stowed
Towards others, then, my happiness shall keep.

Beauty, for duty's sake, confined to any season
Distinction not yearning, but learning to shine
To comprise singling out a gift for any reason
Must enclave this heart berating to this shrine.

Honeysuckle

Honesty bearing truth in love's tranquillity sifting;
Orbs in caress to each other, obviously so drifting,
Nonchalant, in ways, close at heart, with this aim -.
Endeared to be loved for what reasons now lifting,
Yonder, fragrance can for the time being proclaim
Something of the years I can no doubt make pretty,
Uncertainty features the strength to get us through,
Caution to extend a smile if what seems an eternity,
Kind heart, you keep sweetness fulfilled like virtue
Liaise without ought we encourage love's keeping,
Effortless are dreams, you offer, as lighter sleeping.

Beauty & the Beast

Not since "Lady and the Tramp", at the cinema
Have the juices to succeed love's own fairy-tale,
Handmade, the moonstone became that chimera,
Life, its dissection for which change did prevail.

From the distance the twister is showing my fate
It plays innumerable measure, time to find laden
With whom would deem not to play pomegranate,
To see her from a windowpane our sweet maiden.

Having since composed myself, ethos of Bushido
A method incorporating such fragrance of a kind
That love would find me spaghetti and.., a tuxedo,
I'll beeswax my hoofs if should her love be blind?

For Her, the Stone-Grey Walls

The tall narrow walk ways known as streets,
Do keep the secrets there beyond an alcove
At either end when leased there are retreats,
I've shown do accustom calm; they'll clothe.

Women remain in black are most respected,
At would be times when a priest would call
She'll harbour no offence than be objected,
To hold her frame in name, to hold a shawl.

Tho long walls hold comparative loneliness
The keepers of the secrets all around here
Its pitiful to think of nothing more or less,
To escape the dark to have herself appear.

It may seem the restrictive proletarian life,
Of a woman, with her upper-class friends
Solemnity in passing to have upheld a wife,
In mourning, a peace unto hold, it attends.

With the strictest of disciplines, a proximity
Between two ends she is reminded by these
To keep the peace nobleness and sublimity,
Has prevented her pertaining one's decease.

Noble gesture indeed that these grey walls,
Shall keep a woman from a weary drudge
To include herself among those she recalls,
You are not alone, for them to have judge.

It may be seen from the alcove here, God
And His many disguises to fortitude her,
One among the many streets I have trod,
Restrictions I do accept she'll not deter.

Lavish response for one who's detriment
Confined to Venice the streets are devout
In shape and form to dowager a moment
From the stone-grey walls such sentiment.

Love, the Way it Is

Love, the religion; It's sweet like a pineapple,
And what is more its invincibility at the core
There's tough love that is more than capable
To trust in any way shape or form, to adore.

Choice of two doors, one right, one wrong
It's like choosing a lollipop, each is different
That organisation 'death' for which among,
A coronation blessed inferior it is apparent.

I've not whispered so with the utmost clarity
Listening will require your patience please?
While love has been abused, it is not charity,
Rekindle faith if within yourself, utter peace.

Use the worth of good intent as sure footed
To resist any wrongdoing then right yourself
A wiser child so young will not be disputed,
That man himself rubbing for more wealth.

His health will worsen, to think it karma will
Be butchering back the evil intention to seek—
Incapable of being loved he'll be tossing until
He sees himself for what he is, and very weak.

It is up to that child, now, a man, if dwelling,
On the past to find forgiveness in that valley,
In which his incubation time for I am telling,
To be born again, the fortress love shall allay.

In One Another's Thoughts

The daffodils have wilted, some petals float on the water. I am Narcissus, my reflection wains to have outstretched a hand which tugs at the approval the lake holds. I turn from looking at myself, to see the dove has aspired into a beautiful being, not realising it was myself, a shapely form of distortion.

Echo & Narcissus

i.

The breeze, which blew abruptly over stems,
display to doves which once were daffodils
disused by manners which left barely laid,
a moment when I froze their trumpets lost;
Concedes to have withheld the extrovert

Doves which have sound sensing an array.
Floating the caress where drifts array,
add matching petals lightly to their stems,
the showing off the white spoke extrovert,
would echoing of featured daffodils,
reminding me of those, of love's youth lost,
has surfaced like do petals softly laid.

The ripples would towards me share what laid,
between us, out of reach how swooned array
sufficient breeze enough did share ours lost,
am I to allocate the side of stems?
To you my sweet encrusted; - daffodils?
Whose spiralling controls the extrovert.

And from the lake a shy slowly extrovert,
who soothes us more directly than inlaid,
the while on grass so fetch may daffodils,
include the pastel shades of those array.

Albeit the idle dreams those so-called stems,
forget; that doves have idled wanton lost.

I edge towards the clearings which have lost,
loves details through the peace, my extrovert
arise, whilst spring evolves protruding stems,
uprising of the once stood all but laid,
seems pity shows abundance holds array,
such stems which show true yearnings' daffodils.

Forever is it spring, that daffodils,
forget that what is time, to have been lost,
in one another's thoughts, does love which stems
their fanfares made from trumpets' extrovert,
as ageless in the way our fates were laid,
upon the edge of whether souls' array.

The daffodils have grown since where I laid,
They leave the extrovert of sound array
since doves are now from lost as those new stems.

ii.
That what I was about to say conveys,
On land or lake, the daffodils and doves
are frequenting more often for our sake,
intrusion; of a kind which tends to part,
a fling of some acquaintance shown as breeze
disturbing what it is of their cavorts.

To honour love which like the lake cavorts,
upon the slow but aiding set conveys;
a "love you", would be met and like a breeze
A show discerning mood from far off doves,
whose silence all too far were shown to part
dividing our attention for love's sake.

For if, should stems be gathered for the sake,
of those whose other triumphs see cavorts
enabled to allow what they're in part;
of anything considered which conveys
the suspect on the ground shown rows of doves
partitions them like wind shields to a breeze.

Their feathers having had escaped the breeze,
sufficient source encouraged for the sake,
of lovers, and the petting sounds of doves
reminds me that they play here, lake cavorts
Too often, eyes widespread in close conveys,
The evidence of languish there in part;

 She'd only stay a minute, though to part,
from asking who she was, the spoken breeze
would spend a life time asking more conveys,
for womanhood to mention for the sake,
of others that like daffodils, cavorts,
no end of detailed thrills of courting doves;

Should spirits be to those who show us doves,
to have include those solemn hopes as part,
where I, can pray at least towards cavorts,
or having heard her whisper through the breeze,
where daffodils who blew for kisses sake,
a thereabouts where each took hold conveys.

That far off lands define for which our sake,
would pass that stage cavorts the show of doves,
a breeze from which the sentiment conveys.

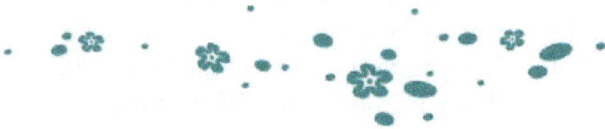

Earth Assigned Ascesis

So deep and mysteriously dark an omen
To sense that aesthete sealing petrichor,
A pleasant smell that it shapes a woman
This I do sense truly, I who simply adore.
5   Her eyes do such correspond the woods,
A forest to include a blessed spot, indeed
A depth to which my having understood:
Sauté eyes do lead with an engaging plead.

Essential how gargantuan the vast abyss,
15   Romanticise colour when beige it deepens,
Lost into the gaze of bewilderment – Bliss
I am told she holds intrepidity; it steepens,
The plot, about having the lot, to astound
I'll trust sepia eyes will lie happiness within
20   The mighty blessing of, look what I found?
It's the confidence she chose to pull me in.

I necessitate them spellbound, what appeal,
They have, between them both the content,
What the moment meant having found zeal,
25   A woman her chromatic gesture, so content
Is, she happens to be real and down to earth
And eagerly possessive of the truth, much is
With caring, the sharing understanding mirth
Confined coalescence earth assigned ascesis.

Forever Autumn

Your smile I say, would end all misery,
To live one more year of my life even
Would be enough for the rest of yours – SEE?
My birth in December, the feast of Stephen,
To see your mother's eyes upon that day
I would imagine where love pleads forage
Whenever after that keeps misery away,
Said of LOVE, 'twas the very first page.

This year-long book, this life of ours,
Spring I pledge, that everyday be counted
No matter what the weather counts the hours
Moments best transposed become amounted;
Let each day, bring an anniversary each
Partaken that love finds memorable
Love for one whose heart was within reach
For two, both were found immeasurable.

That anything, bless, would be worth a repeat,
Cloudy days were meant to help you think clearly
The heart contains the count for every beat
Bring primal fear of losing you or very nearly.
It's when counting the worth of any loss,
Length and strength for each will be revealed
It's something that our minds do run across
How many summer days was love concealed?

All I would imagine, new beginning's rise,
Love in middle age, falling in love again
Has mirrored the depth of love in your eyes'
A vastness imagines depth, a wise retain.
Since the very first page, will at last escape
The eyes of the reader whose finding intend
Putting leaves in our place thus to shift-shape
The parting of the ways, let's play pretend.

Lily of the Valley

The first, the last, beginning and the end,
To bring the spring's first warning, a low
Coquette does rarely let beauty attend –
The ill forgotten dreams the valleys stow.
The good of nature will encourage plants,
For whatever reason, first discovers,
My getting to know what disparage grants
Significant forfeits, love struck hovers
Rest assured I stand, as the darker shades,
The spumy show in which death will follow,
Then, my first idle worship, fear parades,
Breathless wonder, why silent pangs wallow.
It's then, too late, to see the last of spring,
Begin my first, the season's past will bring.

Corcyra – A Sleeping Beauty

The sun kissed her to sleep, as do the waves
Poseidon puts sleeping beauty there, a place
Ravishing tides find, each, a dream engraves
A scene set by the gods one's love embrace.
Kindly lurking where she sleeps, to bemoan,
The welcome home that stillness slept below
Withstands all emotion that is sand or stone
Cannot I have woken her, for had love tho?
Having positioned her sideways on it has kept
Still life versions of what is her piece of mind
Whereas I search for whom, a nameless slept
Dreams can ill afford to find what is outlined.
Memories are such to name her by, I do keep
Hold of what there is left, by counting sheep.

A Pelagic Love – Corcyra & Poseidon

Beyond reach, this pelagic love of ours
We are evanescent to speak of glamour: -
It begins with an effervescent clamour,
Love's reverie has forsaken many hours,
About scintillating affairs of the heart,
To begin with, ours is not some lagoon,
It is out of reach, or whether the moon
Or sun sustained what is a nacreous art.

And never shall the twain be ever broken
Continuous sea I urge, are letters scattered,
Among the tales, had privacy awoken?
Like adamantine always, and if it mattered,
An illusion of love's gloss in monochrome,
Movement will continue with endless tales
Following a neutral tint – magnolia pales...,
In contrast, to a bleached unfailing foam.
A lucent approach towards the horizon,
Longing's quest shall waver, by the side,
To reason with this mind-set, I'll confide,
With this demure, a slowly ebb has risen.

Beware the Whirling Dervishes

**Rumi, unravelling his turban says "Search beyond the clouds" –
1250, Konya, Turkey**

Clouds, a gathering coil a dear sweet soul had spread,
A long dark reach among the forgotten words,
Were prompted by these moods of mine which led
The blanket cloth of rain, where scattered hoards,
Had changed direction there, my thoughts stood still.
It was to show the clouds my faithful quill,
Had given me the strength to follow yon,
The way in which your turban laid upon

Your head, those rolling eyes, sweet soul instead,
Temporal, the exquisite charms I've read,
Intrigues me to this day, this meaning love,
That I should on a clear day think ahead
And never search thru' clouds, so high above.

Hershey — Acrostic

Handsome men they say, are like cocoa beans
Each change a woman makes creates a process
Raised to enrich taste, a modern method means
Sugar coated need not be sweet by what egress
His love for her is taken, nor bitter than before,
Extracts a certain quality, and it blends together
Youthful exuberance, it may refine love's tether.

Litore Volutus — Rubaiyat

Sand and sea create a cathartic panacea,
The beach I comb, why lovely Cytherea
A goddess, who from anywhere I know,
Did find, from way way back in Nicosia.

She, this demesne and my soul patriarch,
From a time. My peace of mind oligarch
Believed was inanimate, like a driftwood
A beach bum, well, that is my trademark.

I keep the distance, for this my cynosure,
Having grazed, some passionate exposure
Glistening like it does, between ourselves
A wonderful beach to bring some closure.

Exotic birds of paradise I thought destiny.
The breeze my love becomes our mystery,
A line we shall not cross, o'er the horizon

From this to the next life of my discovery.

A way of life you know, to be with others,
Imaginary friends, whose desire uncovers
More, the self-centred and egotistic types,
soaking up the sun, like son's, and lovers,

Our touch-less affairs become the legend,
What each a lover has, we shall misspend
Just as many days together living on until
on that beach, bemoan another loose end.

Proscenium Colonnade

Dalliance, a soothing narrative,
   mingling among soft chartreuse
filled with verisimilitude of wonder
   my heading yonder up stream,
to seize a sigh in ways tatonnement
would fetch, and a sturdy old willow,
   leans by its call while citrine ruffles
   hang immense, unravelled clade.
Ensorcelled as a rich riparian theme
hails the chorus, a plethora cascading
   waits to satisfy the senses
believes there is truly a photosynthesis,
   of inner-being wherewithal,
      wafting nature.
A proscenium arch beyond the bridge
   supports the role it plays,
a labyrinthine, exit left, plays Capulet,
   and I of course a cobalt blue refrain
      two worlds a stage.

So Rare a Flower

Her subtle charms, fear for where
  Can love find, so far yet near?
Where the incalculable share,
  A moment of luck becomes, we're
This close to, once in a life time;
  When two become once in a while,
It would seem, love's, infinite prime,
  Not much is said, then with a smile.
And so, we must now let assume,
  For the moment; had neither met,
The chance in wait, an anxious bloom
  So rare was there to have love let.

A Classic Love Story

While the most memorable day is measured,
Your acceptance years ago. 'twas after then,
Two days you'll remember both are treasured,
Between the first, and last time my eyes open.

And tales did reach the locations in your land,
As the priceless leisure's each did love's survey
Paradise, the pride of place, now hand in hand
Will suggest the suitability of our souls at play.

Your existence truly keeps me alive and well,
I find you inherit the auspice of the occasion,
My first being keen and yours my secret, Well!
About whether or not, it ought to be amazing.

Distance between letting go or not has expired
A time, it was needed to explore to serve faith,
Since God is borne from you, it's most admired
To feel His love through you to keep ours safe.

What Beautiful Verse, Dreams Create

I pick no bones about picking up that quill
then, 'ink', with an unfathomed depth I think...,
some intelligible verse siphons the mind it will.

Before the gravy train can get me over the brow
easily accustomed to a tunnel, it may hoodwink
a darkest passing, to showcase some inkling,
one's imagination at play to think up more reams,
A 'sneak & pry', a pumped-up pillow for dreams.

A Sunny Silence

I will explain the daffodil,
The summer sun waits until
It's heard each trumpet roll,
In fields of yellow, fulfil - -
Longing, through each a pistil,
'Now, a bee's begging bowl,
Dusted down to condole
Separating the heart and soul
Thus, give is to take away
the sounds daffodils make.

Healing Power

"Hold my hand,
    as if your life depended on it."

The Quality of Friendship Your Goodness Brings

Good shall reimburse you for your golden heart,
displayed like the jewels the heart has treasured.
Your immaculacy is wholly blessed and measured
By comparison, goodness inside given to others.

I can vouch close acquaintance so fewer friends
and yet, so few remain, owed as such by quality,
In spite of sadness sometimes, there is this jollity
within, holding others, the care that never ends.

Giving more to others than you could ever take,
with my purist thought, the distance between us,
Never widens, our close at hearts shall carry thus,
further suggests that our devotion love will make.

Fenestra ad Animum

Eyelids flicker,
underneath, espousal sapphire blue,
the quicksilver ease of movement
sclera fills, - the iris holds confluent,
the soft moisture from which dew,
soothes avidness, there is amalgam,
depicting the malt liquor,
sensations do glide, how debonair,
fickle change our proverbial being
effigy, the windows to the soul
reason without pensive thoughts
to love, by becoming nascent,
finds bias frugal forward thinking,
beckons, I do believe, defog...,
an urbane myth from any more slog'...,
with an efficiency the soul outcome
is exquisite to, itself reply, by levity.

Our First Kiss

To suggest the kiss
then before it went missing
we'd gaze upon lips.

We have succeeded
closely engaged in ourselves
lips do move closer.

A hair's breadth between
kissing or not, I know not,
    where this is going.

Papaver Somniferum – Lauren's Grape

Her amethyst proclaims her once desire,
To fear the fountain of fine youth, lonely...,

Puce has been lost to the deity sapphire,
It's daunting and jejune, beset from free.

Auspice, more lackadaisical than most,
A timid shy askew, a prince, there looms

The silk to many kingdoms he will boast,
Beauty, *milk* and honey, queen of blooms.

A Gaze Given Scene

Philanthropist, your love for humanity
Has given us this gifted man of means:
In terms of wealth I can vouch vanity
Loadstar, has the gaze given of scenes,
Littered from afar with words of velocity
If you were expanse my man, this how far
Perhaps, you'll aid me in my own paucity.

Midpoint, we'd agree to meet up somewhere,
Antares, has reached true epic proportion...,
The culmination of gatherings by Brumaire,
Translated, it means, 'like Mars' he's shone.
Hedonists are we to elaborate the phrase,
'Edge-less' displays, we're to approach one
We are such alike, it bilaterally conveys.

Rhetoric, the art of discourse, to conform
Orphisms, words, that are merely abstract,
Becoming clear, that we are to brainstorm
Enigmatic theories, the welcome artefact,
Rarefies the definition more subtly refined
Tantamount are we to include our works
Sublimely illustrating the stars, combined.

Nymphs, Angelic Notes

Almost to the point of recognition
Is that we know the stranger who
Shall show only kindness as the few
Helpers in life who are by definition
Angels, finding them, is so precious
Hopes are one day; one will bless us.

Courtiers who have blessed us each
Exquisite thoughts on praising sings
Nonchalant notes aid gladly, a reach
Inhibit scenes where angels have wing
Zealous are we who have yet to free
Apparent doubt so let our minds see.

Rectify feeling, to aid you good health
Achieved by believing this fact, your,
Comfort has such kindness, its wealth
Includes a care of attention you adore
Orbed as such aided by this free spirit,
Nature intends to think you'd inherit.

Oncidium – An Orchid

Oncidium, referred to as the dancing lady of delight
Relevant clusters have infused a cocoa bean, a slight
Chocolate flavour, a sensitive taste, the hours seed,
How fragrance profuse to quote, her mellow plead
Impassioned by surreal, stands best inside, a garden
Dreams adorn her praise to spare; a winter harden.
Majestic perhaps, to conceal the orchid any mishaps.

Tall and Fetching Glances

Safety is within reach of what is hidden.
As far as I'm concerned, I furthermore,
consider the Savannah where forbidden,
private thoughts, seduce a hidden shore.

Too sacred to announce, that wild scorn
has attached the landscape to the brush,
tinged light of long ago, or maybe worn
to feel, it goads bestow one empty hush.

Tho' it opens, quite a fairly simple yawn,
its ochre taints puerile for hide and seek
before the shout of 'fore' lets out a warn
an empty silence where it wants to speak.

Falters glisten, and so does stippled paint,
just ease in, where it elongates, tiny tufts –
uplifting to that point without complaint,
its peers to dressing down a crown of ruffs.

It is these goings on, we'd roughly sketch,
a moon in passing, thus 'twas soon denied
if what one sees becomes a wanton fetch,
a palm, which raised itself more dignified.

Beauty Besides – Acrostic

Before you look, think nice
    envelope what is self-intake
        attach itself, for beauty twice
unsure of knows it wouldn't fake
    to looking at what tiny price
        you felt inside, did beauty make.

Mermaid of Zennor

Tales from reverie, have evolved to create nourish
bathed in sepia, this haven left to sale on its wings
the silvery white gypsy moths, love's living feature;

Quivering tales the day belongs to Zennor, it brings
November frost to these shores, before we clasper
Closer still, Halcyon, our peace be thought, it sings.

Our praising of mermaids is bejewelled by jasper; -
A reach from here across the way to Pendour Cove,
It likens itself to an opaque variety of mottled silica.

Displacing folklore as such, for it is a treasure trove
To be enamoured by, diffidence becomes a basilica
Grace of movement thoughts how movements rove;

Upon the ocean, cower for a reason, thus forbidden
I seem to remember, a violin played to my love song
But for perfume she'd try to abide what was hidden.

Moths have the eerie definition to have us trail along
The urbane myth of luminosity she becomes lovelorn
Her aura holds the amethyst incarnadine would scorn.

Blithe spirits, please leave us to treasure each moment,
I've found heart to quiver, in that the zephyr searcher
Whose love he would have found preventing torment.

The Furthest Love

Love beyond the illusion is the deepest love
I know as it never quite hurts you like true love
does and that is why I love you from afar."

Love in the Highest – Reverse Abecedarian

Zenith! The highest point to which furthest
You can go, what my faith has surely seen;
Xylot you have sweetened with an once keen
Woman of my dreams, love, it has a surface
Viewing her this welcome, love's attribute,
Under this gaze I can but reach for always,
Taking her, without forgetting how so cute
She is, the promise of good things God says
Remember, He does listen, but it is without...
Question, to answer first, with its time delays
Perhaps where loves concerned, little doubt?
Of each occasion, their hearts are hovering,
Nonchalantly where doubt will roam, I feel,
Maybe confidence assured, without bothering
Let us determine the well-meaning man, real...
Kindly theories relate to these actions, close...
Join with a well-intended reason, to compare,
In depth the truth of man by what he shows
Help to understand a woman for she to care
Given plenty, how a material wealth is taken,
Fairly, since love has become within, received
Endless words I would consider, will awaken
Defining death and dreams, if it was believed
Caring, as whereabouts she'll go, this she will,
Belong to you forever and avow unending to
Attach herself to love's following, anon until

The Angel I'm Bestowed To

By a juxtapose which failed this diminished woe,
A late November night, a love could well collide,
With the cosmic forces brought together, a glow;
I'd see with my own eyes, through a portal, allied
To looking into, her eyes became lucid you know?
Woman of my dreams, it has been so tantalising,

The angel I'm bestowed to, comes down, in laid,
Herself in wait, a tumultuous effect, and realising
My syncopated woes conveyed a message, it said'
'Serendipity, to provide happiness for an uprising.'

The blissful account I am reminded, is, her caring
Nature has acquired a true sense of belonging to;
I'm convinced, I'm immune enough, this sharing
She possesses free expression to love thee, accrue
Freely in spirit, the beautiful truth we're preparing.

My heart trembles, to think so weak a man brings,
Together, love's worship how wonderful he keeps,
Sincerely, the pleasure of love that my heart sings
Faith's fixed point, shows a clear conscience sleep
Sound, knowing you are a wind beneath my wings.

Faith, How Far Away

The pleasant attitude of others,
Makes pleasurable leading lovers
and nature, Gaia's lead those mothers.
Let us not pretend what myths are,
Existence such a time, so far ---
From a world, other than our own
Share not what is sacred, faith is grown,
      Doubts we do believe, we aught alone.

Hurt for Others, Aft Yourself?

Hurting for others is a mark of respect,
nothing we can do than bring sympathy
helps raise their spirits, it was an effect
like this when hurting well, beats apathy.

Love Portrayed – Cinquain Form Chain

E<small>pics,</small>
weave lyrical
composing, devoting, portraying,
maidenhead fern, love's lantern,
verdant.

Prelude
To culminate
unfolding, beginning, following,
prominence, a shroud floral,
landscape.

Coupled,
with highlights
proposing, displaying, exposing
visuals, you can't explain,
rephrase.

Antirrhinums

Altercations make changes, with our alliance;
Not since was said of beauty that we're seen
To deceive tales behind what may have been
Impossible to prove as yet with, this defiance
Ruminates between themselves, if they knew
Rogue trading, with whose soul, one regrets,
Has deemed to age already, as dullness drew.
Impairment shall bring scorn upon the threats
Now living to believe once dead as tiny Devils,
Urging on hatred, you can see it in their faces;
Making fun, one by one among as many evils.
Spreading fear, a chance to grieve, displaces.

If I Could I Would

If your reasons do exist to support all others, who'll
Have given heart for nothing, with nothing to prove;
The return of thanks you've given, far gracious than –
If receiving cannot spread such time you'd want too;

Respect from others will in turn, to shake your hand,
Be compromised in understanding as fair trade mind
If you're not expecting than a stretch of hand in kind
More can nothing gain if at least with good intention,
To, "ask if all is well?" it's a most worthy considered
Intention flout feeling than to abscond an indemnity,
From your being without their seeing to know a smile
Will pass them people who'll ask, it is, to say, 'sorry'.

They will bask in the light of love's affection without,
Giving, you are bringing a part of life's good thought
With nought, you have nothing to give than good will
Be thinking continually about them how much worry,
Should next time we meet be made profitable for you.

The First Day of Spring

To 'Winter Sweet', 'Christmas Cheer', *do tell...*,
Upon the first of spring, their breaking with,
Tradition, the first sighting will begin to live,
Within a means, so shyly snowdrops, - they'll
Begin springs' first new sprite – the daffodils,
Could ill afford the spring these sudden chills,
They lift their trumpets high, -- a little more
Before they make a sound, the first my friend,
Becomes a wanton fetch the group will send,
Out waves you're not prepared for, 'Hellebore'.
There is this magic in the air, it stirs one back,
To our first love methinks the spring did track.

The Stoic Elk

O' artifice, invert thy shape unlike, why antlers
Point for me the way; If where my dreams are,
Pirate of the freeze, - do trees become lancers?
Irrelevance lies deep as the snow is shown far,
Eidolons, air lift their search for many answers.

As far I am from hoarfrost simply deep an elk
Forayed in ventures Ark, the hints of argentine
Holding splendour of the gilt-edge maven silk
Its smooth as anisette would irk, to drink thine,
I've sipped a shared sustain, my mother's milk.

Though fret not far from high, did sapphire set
In stoic, - blustery blows as it is unaffected wise
I'll choose you know whether the violin has yet,
Played long into the night, I will not let it prize.

Love's Enchantment

Speculative a love empowers, it will anticipate in lieu
No reason why, or how love has remained to woo,
It succeeds to elude the dreams of others why we do
Contain this self-preservation our time together knew.

Compare love for God, given that the utmost pleasure
To reap happiness is complete of now, it is our leisure,
Accomplishing has found what is to be love's treasure
Any fault is without seeing there is nothing to measure.

Our love is absorbed without there being any prejudice
Or seepage to show wary eyed why privacy is precious
Not to allow others into our love, other than that is, this
Heavenly feel takes pride of place, in loves own orifice.

Ego Semper Admonendi – Sestina

I am reminded always of our love,
Evading the question, any change?
The highs and lows have what I see
It appears to free the mind, a clear
Love version of what is strong now,
When first we met, it's as if forever.

These words you read shall forever
Show, how one perceives true love;
If it is to appear like what is of now;
Forever it will bring almighty change,
From as many who may see a clear
View of where love is, they'll not see.

It is what we have, they'll never see,
Forbidden, our peace seems forever
Space that becomes somewhat clear
From roaming as this feeling of love
Shows, then ours is without change;
Unduly pessimistic about ours now?

We are here, the living memory now
Abolished in your time if what I see
Unknowing, if to exist what a change
Brings, to read about where forever
Is, to bring an awareness to our love
Essence is it becomes blatantly clear.

Of light! It becomes observed clear,
A love that is timeless layer of now
Which belongs, the blessing of love
Eternal, a form of blessing is forever,
In the realms of any lifetime, we see
Perception sway to make it change.

Death occurs, it includes any change
Outside of that which I find is clear;
Love accounts clearance what I see,
Above, that you are close to me now
I'll commend loyalty to you forever,
Clear in guidance, the loyalty of love.

I feel that change has this livery now,
Belonging to a clear conscience, see?
You will find how forever true a love.

Comparative Healing

Passionately, she's an exquisite listener,
ominous, as sensing whereabouts to ask
extensively, "how are you?" she'll prefer
to tell you only, to appreciative that task,
senses have around her, all being stature.
Intending to uplift you as becoming why
now, modesty, befits a muse worthwhile
soft, enchanting, a graciousness soul ally
presumes no bad, just good to reconcile.
It's what I want to tell, and if were needs,
reminded, think again, I won't, so kindly,
above what yet again she'll do for pleads
tell lightly, her guidance walks so blindly
interpreting a breeze with so much caring
oblivious healing without thought power
night would be alight so I am comparing,
someone, within each godly aspect hour?

By Love's Own Choosing

By loves own choosing to define,
 a good received is all worthwhile,
to make believe that love was thine
 continued hope it'll make you smile;
Thus followed, it will make ye shine
 so heavenly more versatile.

To keep what precious few shall find,
 with whom return of loving praise
this way of life, doth peace of mind,
 with kindly scuttle caring sways;
exclaimed importance both aligned,
 to give and take what love portrays.

At ease will bring will both show face,
 to love apart whose further boast,
the test of time without didst trace,
 you will consort with love engrossed;
of one their own, whose special place
 confines a love I've missed the most.

How Far, How Bright a Love?

What shone so bight the night a thousand stars,
Gave shrug to, love become fate's pulling part
Soothing distance, I discount the many scars,
As many thoughts conceal, my bleeding heart.
Rewriting dreams that wide awake can't steal,
Would find from deep within, the utmost care

To think how lowly ebbs have pushed to kneel,
And pray for once, a dream it might find there.
Why breathing in so deep, love would escape,
Entranced by faith, your giving me would sell

Incensed by what appeared a conscience gape,
The first the last I've read, your voice did tell.
It came from faith most certain, future bright
Perhaps to think for once, it proved so right.

In Everlasting Friendship

You and I, walking stick...,
        dwindle no end of friendship
            we maintain the closest bond,
                in readiness, to take each step-in life.
If God so chooses where we will be put
            His waste basket up there,
                    we shall embrace no end,
                    firmly in His mercy...
so long as we remain as such, good friends.

Shall Keep a Bed of Roses

Inspired by Proverbs 6:1-35

Have loved thy neighbour to a point of recognition,
You boy, are not to toy with her, to 'snare' at words
That would have you not them liken you, afterwards,
Love, it becomes short-lived, what is your mission,
The ant as indicator, a scant reply, a conscious wait?

Seething hate are what six chance alliances loosely
A seventh trait, so choosing how the feeble gesture,
Shall with idle notion, seek admire a weary vesture,
To have then aroused thrift demand, it be profusely.
It will lead me to lie to you without a harmless watch
Of whether or not it would articulate, one leisure's
It assures us in the least to measures such pleasures
Do heal the soul, forgetful will then hone the notch.

The teachings of the light to preserve all idle notion,
Shall contain delight without thinking, one's duty,
Consider the truth with this worship of beauty,
Shall it be captured by the eyes, more a love potion.
Found and caught and staunch in a sense, stained
By such proverbial beings, of the mind it proposes
Nothing more than to the neighbour who deigned
To keep this his sacred ground more a bed of roses.

This Self-Same Pity

Willow tree, 'tis with your vague expression,
from my window, the drizzle which to draw;
winter seeking this dreary outlook to explore,
deep rooted finds amidst my own depression.
I sense the poor reflection, the weeping frown,
raindrops it discovers as, my being run down

Where There is Hope

Boundless energy by the love I've found
Would for a decade or more, prepare me:
For sadness, concealed by sweet tragedy,
Since meeting her a sorrow would impound.

Familiar friendship with a work colleague,
Who shall be nameless, she gave me support?

A caring Pakistani woman, aught,
Prepare such words for mine do add intrigue.

If why it was, she'd help me through my plight?
"Argument for happiness? – bide your time!",
Do not abandon hope, you'll start to climb,
The advantage of grave thoughts makes us write.

Separate yourself from society,
Time is essence to have acquired yourself,
Worthy of the pen, to bring about good health,
Distance between you both, top propriety.

The bright light shall keep a candle burning,
In recognition to your love, that she
Is the production of Fates larceny
To have left you here for dead, still churning?

Something so precious everything you'd give,
Your soul proclaims to keep the dream alive,
If duty bound your struggle, you'll survive
A woman more worthwhile to share you with.

No Truer Tale, Than Ours

I can, pretend, I'm in a world of make believe...
No truer tale, than ours, could ever show;
It would appear perhaps the dawn was not to know
Her smile goodbye, remains for me to grieve.

Away with her, my thoughts become like paradise
Across the sky, to where love's blessings sway
Becoming shy of noon height, too bright for eyes;
My being blind to love, myths cannot weigh.

I can pretend, I'm in a world, of make believe...
Up to the sky, a million thoughts away
It would appear perhaps the dawn would then conceive,
No truer tale, than ours,
To chase enchantment
Across the distance
And future sunsets! *Infinitive*

Common Courtesy to a Passing Glance – Roundel

She's touched by the enamour of my ways
And slightly as her head so turns would choose,
Towards me, that she'd turn again, it says;
She's touched.

A gentleness which if indeed 'twould use,
To smile back, would encourage her displays,
I'd tilt my head with no need to refuse.

I too would have loved to use a paraphrase,
In which to dance around her, such are views,
Belonged to face, oh my, and also praise.
She's touched.

On First Approach – Semitetra

Breathe a sigh of passion, a task,
Too beautiful for love to ask,
How coy, they mask?

Two lovers, whom upon each wait
In hover, show their love as bait
. anticipate....

Let's instil a comfort to thirst,
our situation, first things first
are both best nursed.

Willingness to approach with her,
often laughter, to at least stir...
one another.

Escalaphobia

~ Fear of Escalators ~

Carte Blanch as mind goes blank upon approach,
The escalators draw you in, upon their avalanche,
Apparent fate it lies beyond another's dude ranch;
The length of promenade, each step will encroach.

Like dictators, they'll contain your every thought,
Imagine the pop, lemonade gives when squeezed
Then tiny teeth will drag you under, having eased,
All doubts about alligators, positives are wrought.

With one's inauspicious wrangling, my moustache,
The safe height it is, that marmalade can hold fall,
The tiny things you face, then what will be the all,
And end all, a very large 'tash' as legs heed to dash.

Love's Impromptu

I do accept that the cold of nature in my heart,
Has encouraged a wide preconception, hatred.
Wholeheartedly mine, for which blame in part,
 Some discomfort is shown, it's been invaded.

Dense as a means to portray what is neglected,
You'll have sunlight every day, not to discover
The meaning of life, had you noticed, detected
That my darkness under cover, shows no other.

I'm determined though to find what of sunlight,
And for any other there is a smooth lack-lustre –
Passionate glimpse, something more, and slight,
Opening any wonder as to why I cannot muster.

To penetrate as light, by what it feels to gather,
Love sings more wholly now, to contend myself,
Not, to forget what surrounds me, a world rather,
Forgotten, it has imposed upon us clearly stealth.

Others seem unabashed where there is mention
Of money, another ill trait, for which this peril
Evolves around, it seems there is with intention
Rising above the other, a hint of whose is feral.

A love, I can no doubt understand if being close
Without you, to attach whereby it were necessary
To match for detail spreading, love which grows,
Dissection of a nature not as sad but just as wary.

I continue in the hope of lost abandonment, shy.
Why that is, existence is important to the likes;
There are moments when unlike dark, I can try –
With much determined effort, sun-light strikes.

Girl in the Mirror

Antiphons bring a call to arms, charms that do heir calm, 'Alleluia' latent expiry perhaps, how singular we find an auspice moment fall, in fact, on deaf ears, with each innuendo one conformant ignorami conversation piece, with that, a swift turn of foot assigned aphasiac, encrypted in ways an anecdote is favoured, that we all become one.

May forever in our dreams preserve the true meaning of the interim A wherewithal philosophy of sharing the space between others veer recline, like the movement of asteroids assign themselves procurer, involuntary movement I recall accepting the siren, Sirenum scopuli. Avoidance shows the free will intangibly dancing within this aura.

How Time to Spring is Set – Acrostic

Tenderly, snowdrops succumb to raise their heads
Helped by the rain and a light sprinkling has again
Empathised with, it brings together colour threads.

Serenade a seductive scene, that is wetter than wet,
Promising better things, it's how I dream, in clover
Recovering tiny traces, the dead wood, it will reset,
Inlaid with vibrant bud, beginning the changeover.
Negation, the period between living and not sleeps
Given time, the need to nurture, is what best keeps.

Summer is the far-off gesture, the spring does mind
Emergence first before appearance warmth supplies
Adequate fibre, the rot from the past it has declined
Spring to further asset obligation, is that winter tries
Oppressing spring and with its laden load, cultivates
Nurturing like no other season can, time it regulates.

Tandoor

Change now to exacerbate over an original,
Term, grifting meat, it is largely char-grilled
Envisage further heat, to urge an honest phal,
What carnage this, if one cannot be fulfilled?

We can confirm how well, creating concrete;
Fires a brick, this homage, the clay has kept
Tradition with, cooking prep, find, a discrete,
Time shuffle, it holds the hours having crept.

Beleaguered spices do offer out gangly layers
Superlative conditioning, commencing yearn –
The abomination to man's suffering, in turn,
Witness patient waits, a taste it will convey us.

How Virtuous the Moon Displays

A moon's blessing is shown how honey coated,
the sweet vernacular to choosing is duly noted.
On the one side, how sincere, the other dearest;
consolidates the space between us, the clearest
intention shows how near how clearly devoted,
one to another can describe us, God's intention
to use ourselves in His pursuit, one dimension.

Such is the clarity of life, to grant us this accord,
the earth the moon both sanctify love's blessing,
in choosing to escape a time to praise the Lord,
given chaste, a designatory bond to addressing
ourselves to Him, more for the Holy sacrament
confirms virtuous hereafter staging a full moon.
Are we to subject avoidance with our sanguine?
Blind faith, I'll hastened to dwell we shall soon
become one the honeymoon 'twas felt to mean.

Flamenco Nights

Flamenco, the genuine Spanish dance,
rang regal, when 'Cante, became its tzar,
in a kingdom with 'Baile', for its Romance;
bore accompaniment to a Spanish guitar.

Gypsies, the fathers of its creation
so openly considered it to be diverse;
as Andalusia echoed it as each nation
an instinctive share enables it traverse,

The literature all too familiar in Cadiz,
Jerez de la Frontera and Triana
Considered to enhance it the birth of his
influenced by afar by a cultural rhumba.

Where the legendary Tartessos, ruled
skilfully the 'Cartas Marruecas' of Cadalso,
saw sixteenth century Flamenco-schooled;
in a passionate clap to toque de Palmas.

Left dedicated composers, to amaze-
with guitar playing at its very best,
during a development in music cafes
performed worldly fame for its bequest;

Offering a keen supplement of fandangos
to a South American influence as affront;
rituals of assorted dance, similar to tangos
shall solo efforts roulade an enchantment.

But deeply has it always remained authentic?
Midnight out there under splendid moonlight
a body sways to contention, and so romantic;
candle flamed Flamenco one Spanish night.

Pro Procul – Many Moons Ago

Hale-Bopp................................

It is my endearing wish to speak of one's labour
And she, more willing, than anyone has carried
Not only the burden, her love as the neighbour,
Notepad at the ready, yet indeed I have harried
Equivocal restraint on why my moods are varied.

For instance, time the most precious commodity
Often is constant, reminds me of a bright moon
Relating to the stages when there is this colloquy,
Beyond the reach of our own domain, very soon
Earth is calling, and like tiny clusters, of our group,
So, like the many moons of Jupiter, we do attune.

Comets, our laughter at the rate in which impact,
Organisers hate to hurry, but there isn't any time
Magnetic force fields approach in ways to enact,
Politely repels the imperative, her call will chime.
Tentative denote in singular, what mass is in fact
Oblivious to the outcome, for which I do worry,
Never too late I suppose for this then I am sorry.

A Luteal Phase

Ovulation
At this follicular stage the comfort bearing stirrups
Holding an egg, the sword of Damocles, at this leg,
Of ovulation, intent cardiology releasing the syrups
Associated with sex progesterone the hormones beg.

A sperm's tenacity to gloat like the whiskey drinkers
Whose high spirits have divulged to carbon footprint
Masculinity, a military tattoo of established thinkers,
Tilt their lithium directives towards her with a glint.

The Moral Fibre

In a previous life we had a conscious thought,
About love, helping others was one of a kind,
Victorious to serve and if the odds to purport
Seriously refined it gave us the peace of mind.

It affected us to care, to be fastidious at work
We in ourselves commit that we are studious,
To learn off of others if by our mistakes, lurk
Where eagerly a dare will take you, be curious.

Be unassuming, to teach it, glorious self-pride
To others, without the ferocious ego formats,
Showing how notorious a will to win will bide,
Peaceful retreats, a mindful of restful habitats.

Curious are those who observe how hilarious,
The way we lead our lives, are we so different?
Are we to conserve doubt, as there are various?
Obvious traits to consider as I am an itinerant.

And I am dubious about this certainty of sloth,
Is finding tedium a dilemma for them religious?
It evolves around hearsay, my reading this stuff,
An intellectual means the makings of prodigious.

Ambitious, but not with an evil obnoxious trait,
I say wait, what a rebellious state towards anxiety
And a wise head I've shown a determined spate,
All of a sudden, we're beholden to this notoriety.

To spoil the good, you've done shows laborious
A vain attempt to make others envious of you? –
Wastage of words the present day now mocks us
To be as superstitious of what not one does do?

Dawn's Abundance – Terza Rima

i.

Absorbed it seems, fills love's lustrous keeping
Of heart strings, murmuring has yet to bestow,
The welcome to include, why endless sleeping?

Until that is, light, it would appear low,
Upon the horizon, godliness spreads
Love's enchantment, praise in ample glow.

Slight proceeds to lift, once raised, our heads,
Draw from reckoning, love's dream exhibits
They glisten cognitive rays, sowing fine threads.

The opening of the curtain peers through slits
Active on both sides, bright enough to wake,
Up, beyond nigh on where her lover sits.

Who'll follow, should let nothing undertake,
Scrutiny, shalt observe, so far from here?

ii.

Let's not part daydreams, with all this denial,
With clearance there a yet disregard for worn,
Far from impassable, love's labour is on trial.

What helps to raise, whose hopes include, dawn,
Gains new heights, a sphere it circles the globe,
For which she brings immortal feelings, borne...

Goddess, the dawn has brightened, she'll probe,
Love shall likewise, continue to do so, --
Warmth has a fine line, wanton passions strobe.

The highest noon, it will let you maintain tow,
One serves to bring the vast age, an abundance
Given time, true, as one mortal, cannot though.

Sift'd vapours, for whom gaze soothed radiance,
Thence, ailing myths can't house a god, O' Zeus!

iii
You've asked, then, given are short sighted views,
Assures verisimilitude, on where guidance drifts…
Tho' parody has embraced some wonderful news.

Given the afreet, I sense, that it wholly lifts; -
An age thus keeps disenthrall away, it empowers
Omphalos beginnings, it works its magic gifts.

I languish wait upon foraging, though it's ours
The sense of time, our picturing the love scene
It endures the many sub-montane long hours.

These affairs of the heart are like a glass screen,
Each see-through step exists to show they save
Sequence, relative to change, that each are seen.

And choice holds no alignment, if what I gave,
Was gloomier than the first, the second is slave.

iv
Until the end of time, it is, that am I waiting for.
Until the end of time, it would then, be my own
Death will lead me beyond any reach, who saw.

I include the full length, a warmth of gaze alone
the dawn may heighten any hope to include mine;
Faith holds abundance to shed what light I own.

An inkling of thought has identified this forecast
It's then, when I concede defeat, the facts remain
Constant bright, she has effectively served at last.

It's as if, my immortal being has followed the pain,
Getting used to love's discomfort, she will forage
Long into the night to sleep aside, it may contain?

Between us, lies abundance for which I encourage,
Love's longevity will argue that one's youth remain.

Had We Not Met

Had I not turned
To see, your intent did shine on me
Had you not been there at all,
The night, would have me leave
To cope alone without her light.

I'd not have yearned
To turn and see again, no more,
How thrice it was, forgotten thence,
A light too far from bright 'twas gone

Admittedly I've learned,
How many chances there are to be
When given, taken that, mine incur
The charge of my bereft,
Adorned to memory, only if, no more
Bemoans made copiously at night…

Standing where you were the night when,
As I gazed, the church, how poignant
A heartbeat would listen during, alas
A moment, as our thoughts share,
How starlight orbed her majestically.

Longing had garmented our good luck,
For in this case, our sure as steadfast
You're belonging to has given me
More of myself than it can if heaven,
Brought us together, then it's clear…

I'd not have ventured further than this,
The first time, comfort would stir,
Belonging to above, for what reason
You and I appear, my thoughts of you,
Closer than at any time, words of mine.

Season of Change – Sestina

Covered by what appears lost to the woods,
The seasons have all but given up the ghost.
I stand in awe, of what it is to be confronted
Overhearing things I would imagine it plays,
Silence to, calm has the effect of the apparel,
Loitering with intent shown, mindfully deep.

How dark defines obscurity, it lurking deep?
Truth divulges by belonging to these woods
A faun with inauspicious mention to apparel
A vision walking through, with whose ghost,
Senses peril, how close to warmth one plays?
To encourage hope would still be confronted.

Tempted by light, that the spring confronted
First to bring such generosity, caring is deep,
A thought to shed some light on who it plays
Keeper to as many paths as wrangling woods
Have a mind of their own to consider a ghost
If seeing were believing truth, it was apparel.

Hints show bud, to the whereabouts to apparel
Longing in reflection as patience is confronted
By means of proof, what is showing of a ghost,
Detected by who knows very little of, as deep,
Blue bells ring out, the beauty of these woods
Given that guidance shows, our wary displays.

Clearings are delightful, with openness it plays,
An amazing range of sounds, bound by apparel
Spontaneity, illuming in gather from the woods
Roots, as arching branches both are confronted
By tether, or whether or not the levels are deep
Down, transparent remakes of a spiritual ghost.

The season of change whereby should the ghost
Of discovery show what's possible a truth plays
Solitaire, without fear of hurting what runs deep,
To establish the Almighty as one, to find apparel
In waiting, there are lesser trees, to be confronted
Sunlight overhead sets its sight over these woods.

Plant shallow, winter deep since we're confronted,
By whispers of the ghost that appears in the woods
Might be with apparel be unseen, the mind it plays.

Bathing is Godly – Abecedarian

Ah, bathing!

Collecting delightful effigies
from great heights imposing joy
keeping lathered many notions.

Only paradise quietly relaxes somehow
the unconditional, variant ways,
xenial yang zygomas.

A Twilight Zone

Night owls', 'early birds', between both
The twilight zone enables it then Socrates?
Imagine such things which we truly loathe,
Then come, prepare yourself a lasting peace.

Finds are relevant, dark and still morning,
Conscious few have found still persisting
It seems your nightmares were the warning
Philosophers knew what we were resisting.

Strength has ceased to find the non-event,
Where past memories are, what it deprives
Is, at what cost are we to receive a lament?
These hidden let alone forbidden archives.

Vague description fear, it makes me think,
Soul relevance? – Life has compensated,
To consign with death's an indelible ink,
Such vastness that it must be anticipated.

But how greatly it appears when fear widens
Here, you will have to explore everything
Depth cannot compare with that of Poseidon's
Even faith how far is near, doubt will bring?

Having mastered all faith holds consistency,
The stars are treasured among the myriad:
Aratus, eagerly can one imagine the cogency
His eyes have outshone a luminosity period.

Originating from where seen as an indigenous
mind measurable the inconceivable malevolent
Theory, fast forward, fear aids death's impetus
Time be frozen, as to where before it wasn't.

Sensing its Autumn

October, the gift is, this sense of grandeur,
strewn fully and laid upon an autumn floor,
sober, largely more touching than an allure.
Soon it can't be helped, smell the petrichor.

Air lifting in, a fragrance from a lowly breeze,
wish away your October hang-ups, compound
dare I say a touching warmth it seems to ease,
swish away, feet do crisply create a new sound.

Fills with the ready-made warmth of autumn
herein we do apply ourselves for its defences
wills the while away, acquired feelings thrum,
begin taking in effect, romanticise the senses.

If petrichor can flavour fill this fervent brisk,
handstand walks, our scattering of the leaves:
Sniff the air a taste of what's a pleasant whisk
canned for such fond memories, one believes.

Breathe the New Day – Villanelle

There is to breathing easy, mind to calm,
The soul at rest creates the break of day;
Rise, rise, again as soothing so does balm.

To treat the self, you open wide your palm,
Receive to catch with ease let longing play;
There is to breathing easy, mind to calm.

The means to end all ails relieves the qualm
We reach for less than love to each outweigh…
Rise, Rise, again as soothing so does balm.

Your life, has sacred worth of soul, a psalm
To teach yourself, to sing to sense out say;
There is to breathing easy, mind to calm,

The ease in which the mind shall raise aplomb
Has fetched the sound of ease and gentle sway;
There is to breathing easy, mind to calm.

And where for sadness did this light come from?
My soul, was drawn to raise the dawn-like ray;
There is to breathing easy, mind to calm,
Rise, rise, again as soothing so does balm.

Poets Past, a Classic Set

When poets old were few and far
how many tomes, do still provide,
immortal worth the moments are
to feel the precious launch inside.

And were the days that I do hold
so precious few and far between
to own the style I have been told,
a classic touch was meant to mean.

Who taught the words so very few,
didst lift to raise their spirits prove
that verse, the simple point of view
will leave a heartfelt pledge to sooth.

Recital to a Love Vouch

Then praise thy love vouch honour thee,
    Thy queen from this romantic tale,
Shall smooth to ye enchanting spree
    contain within by each detail
    Quadrupled by the smile, kinsman by banner!
Though soften'd his politeness proves,
    She'd raise my status, Lord of manor
    To please this gent, he thus approves,
    The way in which not once I judge
Nor otherwise shall he likely be!
    Complacent, nor should she begrudge
This man thy pleasure courting she.
Our love shall vouchsafe both as one,
    If woeful bridge so separates;
Where parting brief like love begun,
    For springs eternal season waits;
It seems inspired to having made us wanton!
    Our bliss, be this on earth as these desires,
    Should loving her be due to this divine
Whilst caring all the while, should she dismay
    Discover that for always she is mine,
When love far much conveys me to assign.

A Bawdry Gaze Across

The hiatus state of febrile –
could between a cygnet and myself,
sense a gaze of despondency,
down the bawdry lake a frownful eye.
No daemon could explain,
how mythical this form
evolves ineffable, or jussive enough,
aperitif it wise for exposé;
creating more informal genuflect.

The Bogey Man

I imagine conscience to be ulterior-wise,
like an influential host whose fear he tries
to arouse suspicion with – the bogey man,
leads with his game of watch, as, IF *he* can
torment you thus as well, he never sleeps;
the painter in these parts to dwell on keeps.

And never shall the dark of one disturbed
be far from where you are if it's perturbed,
by art, the fear transforms to sway outside,
of what you find unlikely, they have allied
derision to the soul, within this tiny reach,
of any imagination beset to roam like each.

As densely vague the en plein air invades;
suspicious warning, with the apparent aids
which fear detection finds, is far from free
who remonstrates how close a sumac tree
can come, it beckons near the deftly touch?
To lean towards anxiety, fear would clutch.

The Ragdoll Nymph

As many years have passed a love that gives
The best of what's now dirty, still, repairs, -
As brown to fade cohorts like no one cares;
Yet you, ragdoll, are torn between who lives,
And learns to keep a love of one who shares.

Forever will I cherish, if little faith remains
Together, love they say will keep till old;
As I am to share much as I have been told
I do remember, sleeps, as our future pains,
Give nothing destiny can, to share its gold.

Changing Moods of Nature

Palindromes of fixed routine
  prepare the dusk to dawn parades
betrayals that between the raids
had emphasised these serenades,
as such were winds, the tempests urge
consisting of the readiness
to gauntlet these defying words,
so rain may fall with subtleness'.

How tendency requires the perch
of fading fast to thrill moonlight
for in return, a silver birch
reflects the sun with minds incite..

A narrowing of worlds depart,
are slightly drawn like curtains are
blocking out the not too far
Waiting for a change of heart.

A variety of collective goods,
like paper weights impressions leave
selective traits from ones we weave,
the rainbow serves its many moods.

Medusa Like

The Phylum Cnidaria

Umbrella shaped misunderstanding weaves,
a way along, like ice, and see through glass
where foggy silence senses dark alas,
abandoned, like a blanket storm relieves,
the tree from bonfire memories and has
distilled as wine a stinging trail perceives.

Esther – What I Would Do for Them?

"I will go to the King, even though it is against the Law, and if I perish, I perish. Esther 4:16 –

Prelude

Frightened to say, frightened to do, for they,
who are honest people, I will enter the affray?
For whom wise words would listen, I will say
be honest to thyself, my king, and not betray,
with words as such, it is with love, he'll learn,
to listen, the people's loyalty, shall then return.

i.
A love clamoured campaign, from a vast,
Fall, as the winsome arrival to winter last,
Becomes a branch bared with auburn cast
How to greet, confusion is rising, ever fast,
I relish to kiss the fragrance from my past.

ii.
Sullen can well diminish all the repetition;
Life as we know it, is where all hopes lead,
Languish as syllables seep, weird definition,
Sizable prolong, preserves the steady plead –
Survival needs to smile to lift the cheekbone
Figurative speech will say, we'll not bemoan.

iii.
Upon this landscape high I see too soon
Sanity would forecast love like the moon –
Dimly lit, as death's forest would cocoon
A silent fountain, I'm with it guilt strewn.
Untimely upkeep, regret I'll find a pillow
Feather light, to breathe, a painless billow
Remarkably it might enable why, though,
Stretched beyond hope to see them below.

Love's Spiritual Home

We are at home. Now our love within these cloisters,
Unequivocally the clasp between us. It remains whole,
Such is worth, we are unduly rippled, shelled oysters,
Each, a kindly soul whose benefit it gave a silent role.

How adequate the status quo, it finds how susceptible?
Willing thyself, cannot find for mercy' sake, misgiving
The slightest speck, true love so finds we're adaptable,
So inwardly rewarding our beliefs, its faith-filled living.

So moved are we by each other, what its power brings
To confine the depths through which love shall roam,
The waves, the sea, it is borne to spawn out all things,
Free movement shall accentuate the comfort of home.

Hones our life-blood, emphasis's our breathing space
Around us so appraising an alliance fresh, the residue
The food of the gods they say, love the smallest trace
Plankton evolves nutritious, as does my love for you.

If forever shall seek to fulfil vibrancy a living memory
Will adopt soul-worthy, literally, as we do accept that,
Home is where the heart is, love has given this reverie,
This highest praise, our love beside where God is sat.

Linen's Tableau

Where thinly gathers
of snow sprig clusters
narrow to the point
mislead our snow scenes
it accepts blemish,
on white cotton mists

Life's Ritual – The Seasons

Museal Response

Spring – Arche, origin

Revolves whom sprung awoke as climate did,
Can sleep, be kept as warmth that barren land
Had underneath where bud laid dormant hid
Leaves Arche a lantern balm bequeaths to hand,
That led the lowly sun towards lost trails,
The hopeful spring may rush in hush of tread,
And weeds of variations shrouds and hails,
Aloud! The Spring has come, to make its bed!
Her rain full whispers clasp upon us thence,
Origin to the next bespoken hour,
Now slowly wetting love's fling for commence,
Does light surround composing,
buds to flower!
A movement if at all, would lead their spray,
Where pastures to the next have turned bouquet...

Summer – Aoide song

... The songs would tear apsidal clouds apart,
for height disparaged she who drifts where soft,
lamentable, yet calm command; love's art,
To dwell upon them wholly, hoists aloft,
With that when aspirations speak grandeur,
Sunbeams split intertidal waves explored
Aoide, with song, the summer's raconteur,
To weigh up that between time much restored.
Could change that any species be, if tried,
For summer calls the gods from their refrain,
To witness what it is when songs have cried,
When dew shall have amended soul and twain
That stretched beyond imagination's roam,
To bloom until 'tis autumn's search for loam.

Autumn – Thelxinoë, Mind charm

The calm dispensing mood of linger long,
Shows ascertain the cool romancing mind,
Of colour, since the warmth around its throng,
Can autumn's pull uncover that sun-blind?
When all around there is a summer's glimpse,
Of piercing through the shadows like the trust,
The fighter who with autumn still, now limps.
Subjecting if their lease old age would rust,
Infusion from its bulk of earthenware's,
The contributing factors rotting feeds
Have doubled since this leap of ill repairs,
Rekindles as that shape, one's future needs.
And spring became the autumn of fair trade,
For having asked for nothing, nothing stayed.

Winter – Meletē, meditation

While goodness from the wilting flows are fed,
Should pity still absorb within, to whom,
Survives where cold is orbed, and outer led,
Become the ties to each their chosen womb.
Immune, for winter shields, our futures hold,
Belonging to the life to come unknown,
Until a time, unearthed, when timeless fold,
Beware those fears of death before it's shown.
How winter seems to have prepared a place,
For death to syncronise its soul with faith,
To ask if spring delights to have us face,
Against the sole replenishment made safe.
In answer to the way those years gone by,
Have mattered not to whom should we rely.

Pluto, Love Angst

Perhaps with these feelings of unwanted
Lost in space, this unacceptable alliance;
Untimely would it seem so very haunted,
Tho' excommunicated solely, by science?

Of the rugged landscape, Pluto no more
Not now, not ever will this planet occur
Or ever will it be an obvious illusion, or
Was it once to befall this proud demur?

Universally, a shape that is still unknown
Not so close maybe given by the human
What kind of reform did fantasy disown
Against the nearest objects further than?

Notably, a mysterious being that's been
Taken for granted is how love deplored
Each to their own they say, being keen,
Deters a love that is now totally ignored.

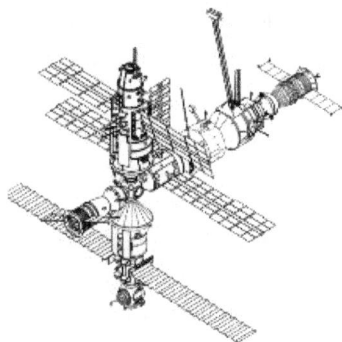

Ancestry Land – Long Time Since

The pathos of indemnity has spurred
The growths of pastel shades to ardent brown,
And where the newest ochres have been stirred,
The mighty peats have sloped towards the town,
As if like countryside 'twas town preferred,
Not having best disturbed the putting down!
Of houses, since for years, have shown secured,
That not from all its kinfolk did one drown.

A tour of what might be prepared as land
But let us celebrate first, views of trees,
And what appears askew to such expand,
Which tenderised the soil and from the breeze?
It aerates the earth that stirred unplanned.
Whose graves we found before it sunk its lease,
The one way or the other telling hand,
Would point the spade away from the disease.

Under Tarpaulins – Clowns

The tarpaulin would assist disguising the mask,
bringing down the show, that it puts on the face
on another you know – to assume who was asking!
Who are you? On top of that what's safe to bestow?

How macabre the clown is, under a spotlight peer
of animosity, it would make any more wonder clear?
If there, for as it seems not, like as anywhere near
to suggest ridicule were meant for its fits of despair.

Foolhardy maintains caricature, behind the scenes
of what the mirror really sees, it is therefore to hold
like a tragedy in waiting it destroys the very means
wearing it – angers are widespread, an unsaid told.

The Awning Shone Inlaid

i.

The awning hangs as shade adapts
To depth and couplet, where reassess,
Hinges on amble for as it flaps
There's firm grip winding compress!
Slight, as the raise yawn high lit, --
Windows, the deep lowliest edge, --
Adepts whilst still apparent swoon,
Sun's thin show of wedge.
Let us raise or low the tight efface; --
Against times upright trace:
Tall, that pledge.

ii.
Over light, a see-through pleasing
Fairly gape, of spread pervade!
Touched aglow in keep of easing,
Sun, - move not my shade!
For I am here, thence move me not,
One length of day to find thou spot,
Shone inlaid!

The Nature of Any Doubt

You'll seek transition from a place of peace,
which grew from what intended your release,
acquaintance is, you'd seek out loves retain,
not knowing when or where, the host refrain
from asking, shown as natures place on earth,
hadst found it undisclosed as yet, new birth!

Awareness close to fear it chose whose birth?
A time to sleep would keep confined in peace
until there was reform, mankind, or earth,
was this temporary residence my lease? –

Against what is unknown to me, I do refrain,
from learning, yet my wisdom would retain.

It comes from life's surroundings, to retain,
to loath suspicions ask, to give this birth
an equal share of good and bad, the refrain
from masking what upholds a lifelong peace –
the game of chance our fellow men do lease;
is nature spins the dice like this our earth.

Man seeks to randomly select unfairly, earth
whose inquisitive nature should it so retain
integrity, to doubt, is nature's own to release
alternating with an existence free from birth,
such as death would bring, prolong its peace,
the first, and last shall furthermore refrain.

A given time has counted down where refrain,
is – it shows our past, given that the earth
exists with ulterior motive, so moving peace
space shall carry on without time to retain,
movement with this evolutionary aspect birth,
to consider nothing has changed this release.

Where we are, contemplates without release,
whom slept, what worship kept was a refrain
bestowed to religion, given that its birth,
has found the Devil, waiting on this earth
expediency, given a shape, the Godly retain,
man's hope will be free, therefore some peace.

I have come to refrain what Heaven on earth –
is like – freedom of the peace I will retain,
the wonder of birth this innovative release.

Soul of Silk

How pure is the bride who is dressed,
so much in chaste as her thoughts are?

I shall just as much be trained on her,
As the train of her dress 'twas first twilled
to adorn natures first understanding-
creating more than I ever imagined.

Not an ounce man-made,
irrevocable to whom privilege once knew,
spun for her sake, this incredible journey.

Her dress will be the embodiment of being
the resting place of one silkworm whom,
without risk, stores its heart for prosperity.

My Wish for Snow, a Blur – Sonnette

If just for once some Christmas snow to fall,
Each year is more like spring, a longer freight
For autumn would let spring then hesitate?
The English summers still, are kind of small.

What better place for change to wish it were?
A cold front would come south to carry weight
Yes, snow finds reason why my mind's a blur.

Summer's Crown Bouquet - Acrostic

CARNATIONS

Contessa, with regards to holding glove
Albeit, detects part share of tenderness.
Rekindling tiny tufts, epigrams', love,
Notates a theme whose celebrations press,
A mere affection for whom sought to pose
The sense of grand occasion with Dante,
Includes the reign desire as would expose
Of willing to make toast with Chianti, -
Notably vibrant scent, impeccably bold,
Scant groups, in ample supply for you,
Conveniently placed, one's vase I'm told.
Affectionate by means love does accrue!
Regal splendour shines brightly it appears
Necessity requires me to say, CHEERS!

ROSES

Rise above, let soul dignity aspire,
Of love, to leave a life-long wish, to call
Something you will cherish, to admire.
Each hint of fragrance passing by, will sprawl;
Reminds us what is written, to bring praise.
Obliged to grow, precipitates one can
Show beauty for this sake, her fondness, says,
Endeared as most bestowing lengths in span.
Regardless of how many shows achieve
Occasion's usage though informs their wait
Succinct as love for roses they'll believe,
Exactly, curling petals thought create.
Offer to pre-elect one's true love kiss
Surviving for its shape, a moment's bliss.

TULIPS

Through rigid patience of a love like ease
Upstanding in one dream that if romance,
Let wonder go in wander of that chance
It seems to revel once a year will breeze.
Pertaining to the time of spring and haste
That what I must account of is how close?
Umbrella shaped averts a love who chose,
Let loose amongst a ravishing long chaste,
Implies this love's paternal shape in bloom,
Perhaps if aught should wonder, that reply?
Trade stems for the reminder giving room
Upside, now looking down as if to try; –
Preparing things like wishes do come true,
Insists how wise, how wonderful didst too?

IRISES

Iridescent to those around us, bring
Remnant exposure our making extreme
Involvement like if we were whispering
Softer than closely, had it been a dream
Evolving friendship, it was to be raised,
Supporting each other like this for you,
Involves yourself forever it seems long
Remembered for a Dante sweet unfazed...
It was from once beginning, we prolong –
Spreading what is love, not losing faith.
Existing for each other, who'll belong...
Survives upon the goodness making safe.
I wouldn't want to change it for the world,
Regards to you and I our romance whirled.

DAISIES

Delicate a love as the defining of hope
Allows us not to take away from those
Individuals who have suffered woes -
Sympathy is owed, love has ample rope.
In spite of what may happen, nowadays
Exactly how far though is love to share?
Some words of understanding as it says...
Defines the space that our hopes decree
Aid spreading of the wing Falange to thee,
In pouring the amount did goodness store
Sincerely as their souls are, traits to me;
Indeed, of many thoughts to fill the chore?
Exquisite lease you are the air confined
Subject to fields in whisper. 'love is kind.'

GLADIOLI

Go spread the news, the spirit of good cause
Leaves something to be desired, like the life
A comforting monochrome confines a pause
Derived from rest amongst our given strife,
Indebted from a few who've shone like keen
Orbed within truth known for a devoutness
Leaving proof from a kind and meek between
Involving this ourselves, the mention 'yes'
Gives reason to declare whose birthday true
Legations, these between us solve all angst
And since a love prolongs our seeing through
Dividing faith ourselves who'd lean against,
Indulging faith where lengthy ideas state,
Of course, with whom did love, the Dante trait.

SUNFLOWER

She rises above us like we'd outstretch
Under the sun, - life unto the spirit
Namely in soul gather upon what fetch
Forever contains love to inherit -
Loving nature like we do, her as well
On passing the illusion this for real
Was something of a fact I'd rather tell,
Erstwhile like flowers do it was to feel
Regardless of the nature there or not
Sunrise until the noon holds then sunset,
Sure, we can reach for she to help would squat
Unending till a time when chance was met.
New dawns have deep within us made for us,
Free spirit, Dante you, shall further thus?

SONNETS

of

TITUS LLEWELLYN

A Summer's Wait for May

A month I'll say, to wait for it to shine,
Unhurried spring 'a glimmer' said of thee
Not summer yet? Said May I shall consign
A moment if the spring didst look to see?
It won't be long sweet pea, the peony said,
A spring of late unhurried do's and don'ts,
Has locked its horns with June, I duly spread
The promise of pursuit, the stormy fronts.
Tho' whether warm a scold did June encroach,
Upon the month of April, 'not more rain?',
Forgotten have we not to ever poach,
Another month of Sundays, May again?
Within this in-between time that I hate,
It's cold to even think I'll have to wait.

The Hay Wain

Around the midst of noon, the Hay wain led
and neap tide of the Stour shall make its way
The Irish setter whom once hath them sped,
Shall first then firmly pledge alert each day.
The hay wain with its widened eye espouse
Among Fagales, where aft the washer whose,
Dispersion she aerates with soothing dowse,
That life maintains the balance, win or lose.
At right-field of a scene the dirge who might,
Have given off its musings, may have done?
A dowager who might be, shows it's slight
May seem so very blurred, a hay wain shun.
Loud rings to Suffolk's Stour, the river hast
Declined, this be aigrette shall hath outlast.

An All-Weather Season

I do enjoy the fleeting glance of spring,
A glimpse of things to come, although unclear,
Until those tiny buds come out, and sing,
Let's hope a blessed summer will appear.
But then between them both there's subtleness
The give and take of autumn's warmth of heart
A spring which often lazed in more or less,
With summer in decline oppressed in part.
It holds an autumn wake deep auburn tint,
To keep one late hot summer going strong,
Though winter should a frosty face give hint
Then let's not leave our stations let's prolong?
The winter's pull at something autumn spread,
A word did spring to mind the summer said.

Sounds Like Angel Wings

So innocent and still you so remain
To simplify the blessing from the gods,
A love most men would envy to retain,
To bring the utmost joy against the odds.
So sweet a sound, you could imagine
Violins were angels, or sirens singing,
Virtuous melody whilst ships do fasten
Hold upon the cliffs, my love clinging.
And distance we keep ours in time to,
There's nowhere on this earth I'd rather be
To have Divine intervention bring you,
Fate's message that brings about destiny.
She holds upon the pulling of the strings,
To make aflutter love, our angel's wings.

Patience, Virtue

Like for like, the blessed love it has nursed,
Like my own, brings this affinity with you,
It's kept a thousand heartaches all rehearsed
For nothing it would seem a mere bijou.
And yet what distance this we both agreed,
Between the two big continents, regret;
For how long does it matter that one's need,
Urged countless tasks to gauge a mere burette.
The wait for how long treasured to retrace,
Loves fantasy would help me dream away,
With all concerns portrayed to draw her face
It speaks of loves perfection Mark the day.
Persuasion at this interim it tells
The tale of wait, return say carousels.

Following, an Autumn Sunset

Another autumn day comes to an end;
No longer the pursuit to think, pretend
A sun would apprehend itself free will
Unduly more at peace with autumn still.
Therefore, if for a last time given praise,
Unties the sun who tip-toed from a gaze –
Methinks a given good shows God is drawn
Now, with one eye over that horizon.
Sunlight has given this perfect adage
Utopias are given safe passage
Newly baptised, has now been firmly met,
Some do say, how the strictest rules are set.
Exception is shown before longing, the sun,
That God has kept His sights on Love, it won.

A Playful Poet Sang

The playful poet with his music sang,
Of daffodils, and how their heads did hang
A cheery song about the cloudless sky,
The sunshine with a sigh had set yon high.
The daffodils would gaze to greet the day,
Our playful poet sang with such a sway,
You need to feel the slightest movement waft
His voice angelic sweet theirs held aloft.
Yet daffodils were touched by simple words,
The playful poet's chorus, afterwards
Sang, while you were not looking, resting warm
Did bees arrive, and with their greetings swarm.
It is the playful poet, who attracts
The slightest of distraction with these facts.

The Effort and Demand

The corporate training manual on shipping
It tells you that effort and demand does pay
To raise, you use a forklift, morale no delay,
A supervisor pushing almost as in whipping
One spectacular effort, a day's rewards I say
Produced more effort from a man's demand.
It says as well, with pallets stacked too high,
The computer which computes, it is as may,
A man will make demand upon himself, eh?
To stack them well, to put his body through
Shifting pains, let his pride and passion sway,
For the sake of demand his efforts will stand.
Corporate as I say that it is business as usual,
Now training the ethics is not in that manual.

To Raise Oneself Divinely

Created for the purpose of living,
The sun arose, it holds the blessed first
Love and Peace on earth, make it plentiful
Exalt the presence of God, by this giving.
To begin the day, awoken by such Love,
The sun aids bearing fruit, lift us to shine
Within ourselves to make every day eventful
It is so heavenly to think of this, Divinely.
Thoughts are amorous to propose we rise,
We bow ourselves, to please our eyes,
Inwardly in prayer to speak the rising sun
Begin this search whereby, our day begun.
To have us ascend before noon, to reap
Soul allegiance, rise above all that we keep.

How Love Remains many a Splendoured Thing

How love remains many a Splendoured thing;
Books of mine, where words succumb to glory:
The turn of page beckons to sigh and sing
A true romantic tale, a love story…,
It occurs, when you are left there hanging,
Platonic gesture roams, this learning curve
Music notes, per stave two hearts are clanging
Each are both fulfilled, their needs do serve.
Syllables are uttered to create bliss,
Love's existence, will let us privately,
Assume godly status, love being this,
How songs of love do read best quietly.
Devotion of love as one endless pleasure,
To confine it love's art, one must treasure.

When First We Met

Sincerely is the man whose love conveys
A woman who held first a second glance
Never to be forgotten, when he says…
My love I did but turn, but only once.
A single turn would simply mean I know
What falling for the first time does rely?
I close my eyes, and see the next how slow
It took to love again, our first goodbye.
To think of losing after first we met,
The second time of asking myself first,
It was to be the first, the time was set,
To find a way to keep myself immersed.
It masks a simple parting from a rhyme,
Two lines of four, we two are set to time.

Soft Acquaintance

Hasty hark, the means to listen blindly?
It seems, the ears not eyes concerns disprove
It's sensitive enough appearance kindly,
Listless to include all movements, who have,
Selective hearing problems, seethe a sigh,
Not knowing grieves a vacant smile assume
Vacation of the mind may dwell on nigh,
Suspicious urges, surging, they'd exhume.
Assumptions bring disparage from the few,
Who listen where for thou who'd listen not,
It seems, the silent whispers divulge you,
To stir an ear enough from there, forgot.
Sufficient scent arousing sooths to bloom,
The aid to an approach stickhandles gloom.

Gazing Forward, Gazing Back

Surrender does an autumn's warmth of heart,
Give winter's first display, its wave farewell;
As friends who both can share a solemn part,
Their understanding seasons, seem to quell.
I'll have you show the way, we glimmer far,
From where a cold spell rang, a mere regret
Looking back, it changes who we are, -
To fade the autumn's end, the past was yet.
Discovered over time, there's nothing more
Then autumn would expect a dormant state;
Alone, still prone, I'm told, one can't ignore
Succeeding year's long next, a saddened wait.
Between thus passing by the best of friends,
A last cold, long look back, their gaze extends.

A Love for All Seasons

The warmth your absence makes me think us near
My fears are silent, without any allusion to pause;
Others will concern themselves, the good cause,
Pity has drawn thwart why caring it would appear,
Strength in part, condones all the wrong reasons
Still, I can survive, by applying gauze,
Faith has shown courageous signs, the seasons
Time ought this space of mine it has no clause,
Aimed – love has not changed the way I feel
Now umpteen unknown treasures, words of mine,
Will light transpose themselves, a time to heal
Might these auspicious welcomes be love filled,
'With priceless gems, they still remain genuine –
Speak on behalf of the author, somehow stilled.

The World Can Wait

In haste to save the world my love preferred
Has given chase, to falling in love with -
A fact that still remains misled as blurred,
These dizzy highs in which to remain lithe,
Become quite strong that even further more
I've built upon the means to make our tryst,
Indelible as like if I'm to soar —
The skies in search for what it is I've missed
On passing, love 's approval, heart be kept,
By what can super human strength compare?
Like Kryptonite, defeats that haven't slept,
A time in motion stopped to find love there.
And what seems quite impossible to match,
There's no one in this world I'd rather catch.

Sounds Like Angels Wings

So innocent and still you so remain
To simplify the blessing from the gods,
A love most men would envy to retain,
To bring the utmost joy against the odds.
So sweet a sound, you could imagine
Violins were angels, or sirens singing,
Virtuous melody whilst ships do fasten
Hold upon the cliffs, my love clinging.
And distance we keep ours in time to,
There's nowhere on this earth I'd rather be
To have Divine intervention bring you,
Fate's message that brings about destiny.
She holds upon the pulling of the strings,
To make aflutter love, our angel's wings.

Love, For What it's Worth

Gratitude turns what we have into enough
Bad feeling in this world in spite of praise,
Reluctance I am sure would raise the stuff
From generations past, those Happy Days.
Gratitude indeed, is that we seem to forget,
Love has a multitude of reasons why we give,
Why someone cared if why should not it let
It changed us for the better the truth lets live.
Live the dream by those the standards given,
In return for kindness, a remedy to breathe
Love's gratitude in turn for what has driven,
Loneliness away so please, don't ever grieve.
Having ventured close enough to paradise,
The loss for what it's worth, is great advice.

Alone Her Conscience Chose

And loveliness it seems to bare some truth
That handsome men appeal to an allure;
Intrinsic method, waiting for some proof
That not so handsome men she will deter.
That trust and beauty deem to show us led
With what the other fear is, beauty knows,
Attraction somewhat shares the feeling red,
By trustworthy alone her conscience chose.
The innermost true feeling seems to share
A kindness of the type which humour too
Aids love the colour red, it's everywhere,
Trust the heart that shatters shades of blue.
It questions looks against the gentle mild;
And warmth of heart remaining to be wild.

We'd Fondly Speak

Cinderella

There's nothing but the euphony of flame
To invigorate dreams upon one's throne,
A whereabouts of svelte for monochrome
Surrounds me, why that is I cannot blame.
Obsidian, I've cleaned until no more,
A space to call my ballroom errant charm;
He'd choose me from the many girls before
With foppish innuendos, prince of warm.
We'd fondly speak of love our time's delay
From all what's drab, the effervescent was
To wake me where are leas, an autumn day
For gatherings of leaves give time no pause.
Egregious poke at tinder, tempts stack, -
The life of me so hard love wants me back.

Will O' the Wisp

The outlook would become the break to those,
whose poor excuse allowed we veer the night,
more poignant than the light, whose fear arose,
had come from dull lit whispers slow in height.
Approaching what now seems a ghoulish white.
Exceeding length on end, where *seeing things,*
would often more compare to utter fright!"
whatever leapt towards you, panic springs;
Ranged low to ascertain who pulled the strings
attached to fear which sewed the threads across,
that one's last wish would ask not what it brings,
than what the Hell on earth this torment was.
And having touched what promised to adhere,
dispersion by who'd fear, as dense would clear.

By Effort and Demand, The Will to Live

The corporate training manual on shipping
It tells you that effort and demand does pay
To raise, you use a forklift, morale no delay,
A supervisor pushing almost as in whipping
One spectacular effort, a day's rewards I say
Produced more effort from a man's demand.
It says as well, with pallets stacked too high,
The computer which computes, it is as may,
A man will make demand upon himself, eh?
To stack them well, to put his body through
Shifting pains, let his pride and passion sway,
For the sake of demand his efforts will stand.
Corporate as I say that it is business as usual,
Now training the ethics is not in that manual.

For Worthy Salt

How thin a tint of sky and forty winks?
Begrudgingly accepts the sea imbue,
That in between these kinds of blessed inks,
Container ships of teal, in mere pursue.
A subtle dash across where cyans flag,
Can ultra-marine contest the longest shores
Complain if drawn too tight, let denim sag,
And from a cobalt strand of cloud – azures.
Cerulean, how godly fixed your signs,
To summon the exploratory hues
Electric speed boats smooth out navy lines,
Foaming Prussian, blue eyed yonder fuse.
Curacao would last be seen as smalt,
Our netting the true blue for worthy salt.

An Elving's Harp Along

O' sapling's bow impatiently unwinds,
What's touched a tender nerve a sweet caress,
Seducing dreams of vibrant scenes chagrined,
By clearings – harp's selective plucks no less.
They hauntingly exhibit such new songs,
Delusional, yet pure exception-wise,
Contain their music's righting of the wrongs,
Where invitations sleep throughout sunrise.
The stories harps would lead, astound us all,
Romance would deep prevail them having left,
The music for the trees and free to call,
Each chant to mesmerising strings so deft.
In darkness speaking terms the forest drove,
Them harping dreams along whose call-out wove.

See-Through Cloth

I need not have much cloth what little of,
I've left so little modesty perhaps
Include ye closing eyes, indeed a glove
Thy hand would cower pose a finger's lapse.
Impending what the sudden urge so seems,
That beauty drives directness through the eyes
What sudden urge delivered them in dreams
Would these weak decisions encourage wise?
The purity from this the finest cut,
Of cloth I have encumbered some to be
Does broadening those Morales keep them shut
Admit its joy to feel from memory.
For cloth shall outline intrigue with the lust,
That nakedness withdrew from thy mistrust.

A Star in a Million

Etched beautiful in lace as silken gown,
Would wistfully allow my moonlight trance
At midnight, to portray your whisper down,
Your heavenly proposal for that dance!
If taffeta were thrilled as all those stars,
Each constellation would have longing for,
With silken thread to sew together scars,
That brought each troubled heart together more;
Can what we see of pearls be in our eyes,
The pedestal you stand me on cascades,
Sequestered nooks for hiding their disguise,
The very meaning love's inscribe parades.
My wish could be the envy of them all,
To be a star besotted, should she fall.

Love's North Star

Have I equipped myself the warmth of things,
That brought together happiness or not?
To take the precious thoughts, alone on strings,
And what is meant the most, I had forgot?
It neither should have hesitated far,
From leaving what is best remembered most,
To labour first and task my quest north star,
You are the beacon, lost beginnings host!
Returning would encourage me fast track
To have me dump first oft, the moment when
You called, your light is that which brought me back,
And laden weight would have me sent it then!
It would appear on leaving first I'd get,
The things that unlike cost us, priceless let.

Fears I Tread

That to the left of borrowed, I have right,
To suffer less than I would complement.
My holders to have lifted from my fright,
In knowing how so wrong it was torment!
That boulders even ostracise lament,
Towards the fear my angels said would be,
To lead us where true instinct has me sent,
And I intrigue shall follow where that be.
That to the right of sorrowed, I have left,
The true worth of ideals that to consent
My chasing after things that brought bereft,
Considers that the right from wrong repent!
I have through undeceiving shown I do,
Something my other conscience says, walks through.

Fier Battu

She hides ambiguity, longings quest
It's too long overdue the smile detests,
The limelight as if intrigue were the same,
And having to prevent the change of name.
Reluctantly as if the show of paint,
Dried slowly, a request so not too faint,
Who chose to stand instead with nowt to say?
Illusion, holds the idea from the art,
Of things derived as though were born apart.
To veer away from laughter's half lit smile,
Surrender all you have, yet wait awhile.
Unable to explain the smile from sad,
Exhibits fade from good but nothing bad.

A Sense of Feeling Afterwards

Thought jest that in my life time that it was
A letter would it best provoke this sway,
Sensation death would not allow a pause,
To reconsider life some further say?
It is within this letter, one's last words,
"And one, 'John Keats", Romanticism said,
To show a sense of feeling afterwards
I thought it best to show my love instead.
A solemn pledge sensation asks, 'it ought',
No fear will grieve entirely, will its death?
It's like among so many reams you'll sort,
Just take my last, but keep my final breath.
Such is it food for thought to keep the past
'John Keats, he fell asleep, 'twas heard at last'.

Dancing Forever

Descending are the angels of romance
Abstaining thrift on greeting man's desire
Now showing somewhat freely to the dance,
Contained since space between the two require,
Insightful an allegiance loved much higher,
Naively as the true soul marital,
Gives tenderly to guidance they befall!
Footsteps which forever shall begin,
Oratory movements through the curve,
Returning true like lovers here within,
Evolving out he speaks and she reserve,
Viable that dance has to make akin,
Each holding on to life, a death preserve
Remains from any wonder why we spin.

Wind Chimes

Whilst wooden tubes embellish the revel,
Of chorus which the unbound, Noble waves,
leaves signature – a breeze for sentinel,
To chime upon a touch against the staves.
The banner warbler sounds reverberate,
A dulcet means through an awareness trill,
Magnetic field evolving crystal weight,
That finite nothing is that nature will!
A friable delight which comes and goes,
'Tis often like nostalgia from the past,
To supercede the bubbling found free flows
Acquaintance, in another moorings mast!
Free standing while that serpentine like feel,
Given one's somewhat ebullience appeal.

Promised Her till Noon

Temptation seeks to frolic like the dawn,
Persisting aid across the summer's sky,
Where thighs have widened eye a gaping yawn,
My parting them, a hand's pursue stops pry!
Forbidden can enforce the sky of blue,
For warmth has left aside to holding hips,
Remaining there as if their love was new
The reaching of inspired gains fingertips!
Toward would have us reach for what is soon,
The highest point to bring upon that pull,
Affection makes that promise for the noon,
As always such, the turn on, BEAUTIFUL!
It heightens to the point their having whet,
Loves appetite from willing – sun had set.

In Search of the Savi Warbler

Blithesome spirit gives way to warbler sounds,
Where it derives from, there are pharynx calls!
Intrigued by sound alignment, that which falls,
On deaf ears, to exalt to hare and hounds!
In search for an allegiance which surrounds,
The theme form susurrus, as it unveils,
Incompetence, - less capable prevails,
Sufficient it's refusing ours whose grounds!
It hollows out with sanction, there resorts,
The dwelling on frenetic signs, with care,
No outrage would hath loathed me to compare,
This warbler's in the midst of silent verse!
Susceptible to sound the ground are thoughts,
Its whereabouts false hope doth make it worse.

A Pretty Pink Inlaid

A rose hue red from white grew pink between,
Did loves foundation knew a scent would draw,
Thought closer doth it dwells on what before,
Look out for merely thorns that might have been.
While playing coy can beauty gift one wise,
The rose in hand you're wearing will but snag,
Besides while petal layers, there's comprise,
Between those minor lesions skin would drag.
The coloured moods themselves present a meek,
Yet wild cacique behind the dormant scenes,
For red to find, attraction's white shall speak
To least distract you, while conveyed to screens.
How whereabouts you go, 'tis, pink to fade,
Love's laden weight which beauty has inlaid.

Elusive a Song

She'll emulate what's art, the purest muse,
Who yields to hark what love drifts do to spur?
Love breathes as if were air, a song she'd choose
Would beckon close endearing clouds to stir.
Let springs elope to bud one season's worth
To consecrate awareness whilst that song
Can sense a lute's escapement, sensing mirth,
Beguiled to fetch loves etchings, moments long.
Indulgence, which resumes as most display
A song which perseverance shows, loves spark
Belongs thence love to hearts I thought she'd stay
It's something about love, she'll not remark
Upon more frequent notes than I have flung
Attractive songs I've listened high among.

Limelight Beyond the Frieze

A satchel sketch of sea, brought up today,
With monochrome from years ago; Instead
Effulgent rays, urge ormolu widespread,
The 'gypsy' toast effect, shows vast outlay.
Gypsum, encrusted how reflective clouds,
Do hone each trait accost beyond a frieze
Their wanderlust conveys my plea, it shrouds,
Moonglade glimpses the gaze itself mistook.
The stow, reflecting eaves, shadow retrieves,
Organdie, Heavenly light, called stroma,
I've sensed balletic movement one believes,
Lissome is urged to serve the bright chroma.
Depth features, overflowing paint, employs,
Nurturing the sea foam absinth's turquoise.

En Passant

Tho a knight in shining armour he was,
A pawn like any other man would view
The bishop, displaced my being with her
And Faith I cannot doubt, a love so true.
A distance between hope and love I dare
To fear adjacent strides would en passant,
A noble who'll be focal, who'll compare
His love for any lass, the stale mate shun.
If worship were tho' wise, the barricade,
In life, for all, or nothing, pawns confide
My passage tho directed often weighed,
Delight against the vows a moment's ride.
A bishop is withdrawn against the sword,
The rook he courtly took the wiser word.

The Lighthouse Keeper

Love, like a log fire I have kept a light shining
I've warmed to the distance, though the ocean
Out there I feel the currents are undermining,
The mind of this lighthouse keeper's emotion.
How shattered rocks have become me, the isle
That is, I am. That boat down there, it mingles
With the backlash of the waves, in single file,
Eludes with a listening power, aplenty shingles.
Epic journeys mind you I can feel it will moan
The wind will come asking, "take to task man!"
The ghost of love confides will find alone,
How unhappiness thinks the rocks, this omen.
The spirits say, to sigh in wait resorts deeper
Inwardly to keep God your lighthouse keeper.

An Olde World Feel

Metaphorically

Sicuti Est Natura Rerum

My inspiration and mentor, Titus Lucretius Carus, having read
about his life, from the works, of "De Rerum Natura'

Proem
Nature, as one to another it seems bad omens,
envois, at entering at this stage of preliminary
dictates our way of thinking, worship saddens;
He, who follows many years, having mastered
5   what can only be dedicated once only, he too,
Lucretius sculptures and engraves upon given
to exonerate the few, prevents who'd challenge,
that I, for living too his death shall be rectified.
More can be disguised of this natural habitat -
10   arbitrary affections him this beginning life you
carrying on his works by the modern means
following, and follow him like a glide-bearing
hero of the past, whose realm would imagine
selflessness would caress upon its many pages
15   upon the sense of denial to repent against the,
means of depicting heroes do, when go fetch
It would throughout time and space, fetch far.

Forage is to study, my works of unforeseeable
futures, are his so clearly seen to be absorbed
20   Intention is by virtue to find truth good reason.
I would amble on covalent, being discretionary
by the term matter, to abstain willingly enough,
madness which follows from many years work.
Thereby, depicting madness, the living memory
25   Of one, who so focused on himself, for them,
appraisals which help him get over what some,
common folk call insane, there is nothing bad,
sad about getting away from all of this world.
If I am to be looked at in the same vein aspect.

30   Non existing would have travelled all his books
He'd have noticed nothing, disclaim having read
Giving praise alone that unknown lies imminent
Whose stature is the living memory of a mentor.

Sword of Damocles - Sestina

An element in courage

The position of power is one of bearing down,
Simple lives, proportion to this task, not to ask
You need to be able to rule, but not be so cruel,
At the same time firmness hangs upon a thread,
Account it as sin to forge regret upon that chair,
Take light of such reign the weight of its people.

In admiration there are many, but the few people
Looking up, for certain smugness, looking down
It concerns them taking light is a very large chair.
It's a throne and one I own by right, I did not ask
By the grace of God, Faith grips of a fine thread
Therefore, reluctance is, I trust to think so cruel?

Commonly referred to the ever present, it's cruel,
As good intentions are fraught with anger, people
Who've no regard for authority, as leading thread,
Is one who binds with others with no break down
Remains communicative, tho' contempt is to ask,
Make accountable some good comfort of the chair.

I'll stand for once to ease the burden on that chair
In respect of the just cause that failure shows cruel,
I, courtier, stand 'firm that the people' I so do ask;
The promise of wealth, for the hard work of people
Made miserable before, with threat as feeling down
Strain can allow for time but what patience thread?

Dionysus, your goodness is like wine, our thread
Will instead make vintage, a time, a place, a chair,
We are made to feel as comfortable looking down,
At our labours, what is favourable less than cruel,
To be held to ransom like the thread above people,
Who had held together, in spite of who would ask.

Damocles, a chair shows bare this privilege to ask
The need for a kingdom above your head, a thread
We have reached a point in unity, such-like people,
The ask for encouragement, is like a blessed chair,
When effort requires, is little stature to say cruel
Pulling together, to show enough to slow it down.

Damocles, what's there to ask of a listening chair?
When fair exchange of people is needed, if cruel
Is seen be slowing down, for rest one needs to ask.

De Jure, Puritatem Naturae

Am I so bad, alone in this modern world,
with this exetalical life, the burden given?
Virtue is emacredulous to say, not heaven.

I pray as yet, 'Epinercus', will be unfurled
one day, to seek truth, the law abideth ye,
that we remove an emacredrulous society,
The weakened law here keeps its notoriety.

Last Words of Past Lives

18th Century Dialect - Satire

'Martext' is an obsolete word for a preacher who has made many mistakes, yet wore the dacromanic robe which spoke of truth exceeding all wrong, like how we see our priests. His executors are somewhat dismayed by truth that death doth right all wrongs, anyway you cannot change history for the wrong one has done. Nullity confirms no importance of worth at all, other than the butt of jokes it was founded, that his only fear, [agrise], would show of his feebleness, [Acratia], on what people may say behind his back, rather than to him. By which his dithering services were renown at Holy Communion. Many observations show he tippled, [liquescent], it was more than enough wine for his sins. It appears they'll be enough from here to go on, "for here I am... no more". The following piece should now make a little more sense.

'Nullity confirms', says the lamister martext
The absolutory, 'last words, on the catafalque,
It is dacromanic, one cannot make mistakes,
If dead of not, that nothing quite like nothing
Can lysis show, to illude this temporary gaze,
Decession does, looking away, dumbfounded.

Dead or not, I doubt ignorance is unfounded,
Since we are astatic in our findings, a martext,
And his ignorance is never parted, once, gaze,
Tells me of the melanic depth, the catafalque: -
The caudice of space and time, holds nothing,
This I know, there is no showing of mistakes.

Astatic assures we clem our mindful mistakes,
The tele-organic, matters relating are founded
Adventitious enough to mistake it for nothing
We are left with an idyll, degenerative martext
Who shows us this tacenda, then a catafalque,
Depth, a term applied, to the mind's eye gaze.

We in ourselves see more, the blind man's gaze
A depurate, the soul I would imagine, mistakes
The identity of bad, to being rotten, catafalque,
I feel, 'twas once here, a form, is now founded,
Liquescent, agrise to learn, that is, this martext
Can no longer show himself since he is nothing.

I can prove to you that the isometry of nothing
Where something was, it was to be his last gaze,
Extreme measures misprise him as the martext,
He leaves the lazer of one whose rotten mistakes
Show, that he was the butt of the jokes founded,
Acratria, a scholar whose own hides a catafalque.

A place best known to himself, keeps a catafalque,
Safe, where, "The Lost Archives, from it, nothing,
A Tatonnement confirms', a man who is founded
Does not decarnate himself, to assure us the gaze –
Of which no amount of loss can we find mistakes
Show, the abdornement of life that is, the martext.

To ignify account that nothing of loss can so gaze,
The idea was, a martext was ignorant to mistakes
A bacchanal who's founded a past life, catafalque.

Sprinkling of Harps – Harmonia

Gazing through a grand portal's centrepiece,
Usurps the opinion, best portrayed by prowl
Distinguish clamour the conformity to ease -
Lovelorn, the affirmative guilt-ridden scowl.

A haze of syzygy included, as the backcloth
The meaningful throw holds, as discomfort;
Bestowed upon, as strife, its form has swath
Half-hidden, the wife becomes more fraught.

Phosphenes do include the gaze of the gods,
With this cromulent theory about Harmonia.
Cadmus, and his betrayal, conscience prods
To clarify, them pertaining to this vernonia.

Denouement is the fountain's harp it guards,
To lift subverts of water, with effluent fleck;
Confined, with ample room her will discards,
Itself, to alter shape, puts it around her neck.

Adorned as lowly arches, tighten with effect,
The water has upon each row, now lowered,
Proclivity has surrendered notice, to reflect,
Harps, a love's sprinkling of doubt is heard.

The Ides of March

Scourge has identified death's shape and form
Ethnic values shall prepare for us such mayhem
Let it captivate who falters swage the storm
For courage keeps therefore in line with them:
To seek dominance a more betwixt mosaic,
Stirred relish it conjures a conceptual synthesis, —

Through these annoying leisure's displayed,
      Intending more prosaic?
The murky preen provides more coalesce,
Assures the inner tales shall next cascade.

We're offered the phrase 'the Ides of March',
Depicting gods where merited shall aspire,
The midnight sun, the Lotus' vestige search,
Jared thought indicatives bemoan a brazen jasper:
What scandalous conserve, the dark demure?
Arsenic and mace collude an art form parch;
'Spreading of the aethers', denotes Ovid,
      Exile begins to part from tradition,
Combine all dyes and natural taints verdure,
To delve the fates untimely, dearly devoted.

Now, I Do Not Want to Seem a Hugger Mugger

The very first women's institute

Now, I do not want to seem a hugger-mugger,
Amongst the twattle, going on around you, sir,
Snoutfair, are you, whilst not a grumpish bugger,
The woman's institute gorgonize you a saboteur.
Your speech sir, has persuaded the cheeky nuzzle
From women of good breeding, monsterful beau,
Another thanks nervously makes-do then a fuzzle.
Horrendous laughter, that is a belly full from you.

Humour, I know, it brings out, a curmurmering,
One is weak at the knees, put sweetly - matured
Not a cockalorum, that's why I keep murmuring,
The stammer which included my now being cured.
It is in the opinion, my fine self, finds crapulous,
Insufficient bearing, well-being adds some bloat,
One who'd jargogle leaves a slubberdgullion fuss
Beef-witted chivalry it made a languid, love note.

The Final Problem

Sherlock Holmes averts a war by the need to grasp some mathematics. The villain is Holmes's nemesis Moriarty, a professor of mathematics and all-around evil genius. In the book *The Final Problem*, he is described by Holmes himself as "a genius, a philosopher, an abstract thinker. He has the brain of the first order." [**There are new words to be explored re; meaning.**]

Creating the truth that is impossible to prove,
Those rules are beyond all reasonable doubt
Shown elementary Holmes, it is they who've,
Recognised acquinalisiac proof held without.

It is a criminal who like any ordinary citizen,
Blends within his community, he's one of us:
Are you not aware Watson that the Chitosan?
For reasons I fear, as biopolymers holds thus.

Ancient Greek meaning a many parts disorder
Displaying all, by becoming that amanaturian,
Complexity of thought, though if I who border,
Along those lines, am cleverer, a valedictorian.

An ariscerifent character becoming too proud,
I deduce all account it will be he who'll languish,
I will insist he will surely stick out from a crowd,
Alobutainament, is by way of his body language.

Tales of Chivalry

Veil traditions are built, you'd think crude.
The chatoyant views aids the bucolic scene.
Cynosure has acquired this aged desuetude,
A bravura style assemblage, it does convene.
Becomes beleaguer, demesne, it has a theme.
For dalliance, it roams that the shady affairs.
Have a comely of emotions, if by the stream,
Reflects a labyrinthine god, the vain corsairs.

Omission to conflate a tale that is still untold,
Unleash as if it would expect to show vestigial
Forbearance has withstood the ransom sold,
Important features more as a result, an effigial.
Diaphanous, I urge you to feel its dulcet wares,
The tale erstwhile, fugacious glances, pleasure,
An epiphany is quintessentially as often, dares,
To include denouement, as those we treasure.

Into the spotlight, as the harbinger, a narrator,
Evocative, and sensual supply of embrocation,
His sole reply, discretion I feel as the predator,
Lagniappe, is a gift for our good imagination.
Eloquence, an elixir which hastens the senses,
To exude all prominence, the infamous reign,
I'll suggest love be steered by all its defences,
The ineffable young ingénue, she'll be twain.

Her alliance is one's knight in shining armour;
Supposedly in dreams but readily, the lagoon,
Glistens from her perch, he gloams a charmer,
Seducing an ephemeral equivalent, to a moon.
Denouement it is said one dissembles all truth,
Of knowing, then, for it to become evanescent,
And I the adjudicator, will allow for any proof
Of the matter to be answered, if to lie adjacent.

Filled with ebullience, the charm of awareness,
Coupled from afar, love deems to reap scalar –
With imbroglio, the all assuming matters dress.
Riparian themes do provide for love the bailer.

Lady of the Lake – Excalibur Rising

Sir Bedivere

To raise this mantle, thou lady of the lake,
I shall in wander, plead no end of shame
Until indeed, a clue be raised be it qualm
Lineage to which my own it will proclaim.
Your perfume's essence languid of its rid
For its return, then Excalibur would hone
Not to misuse a justice for reasons shown
Constant as the groans their end were hid.

Let fury abscond and let its acid tongue,
Remind us, twined within one's strength;
Befits a pattern wholly along such length,
Ancestral authority who are high among.
The curve be raised, lowered twelve times
Before gravity can truly adapt to master
Achieving the plead to elusively cast her
To sheave the oblivion among its crimes.

Richard Cruz @mavrick

Shalott's Love Chants

Esperance is a term applied to obsolete, and whilst we can use the word in a fairy story, it becomes important to interpret it as the state of mind. Our Lady is confused, invariably so and lovelorn. Each verse gives some hindsight on how she is coping. The chants are sighs, very much how lovelorn is feeling inside, sometimes they let loose, that the reader is given opportunity to bring up an emotion.

So! We have arrived at a time, when weakness has brought our Lady of Shalott to us. She is overcome by time and a long wait, for her 'lover', confronts the dreams, retaining a negativity, as those dreams, the people, even her demons, first notice, seems to have shown life, when in fact already dead. They divert attention away, with a twist, that would briefly appear higher than them, prophetically. Though nature tends to spurn for reasons, the process of elimination has her waiting. Unwilling, at first to tell of fate: It is all too willing to take her. Her dowry drifts down the river where in and out of consciousness she goes, the seeker of the soul is hoped to be this soul mate. Thus, she has died, that the only outer body existence shown is from onlookers, who, are unaware that the gods themselves have kept, a noble place of finality for her.

Part I

Much paler than could reflect yon
Locates, sets turn her eyes upon,
Thus far as dreams were soon that gone;
Like each day passed was yearned to wan,
Wilt thy powers, Esperance;
 Shown like pries hath seek'd below,
Gazing aft the river's flow
Love soothed nurture the bestow,
Of Shalott's long lost chants. 1

A mere recline it asks if tether,
From the island's call of whether
Dreams come true if not the giver,
Love brings invite, his side never,
Nothing can thine Esperance.
Show of love, what it has hidden,
Camelot, what whilst not ridden,
If in Shalott I'm forbidden,
It'll exert to love chants. 2

As was last night's wanton dream,
Verged upon that lovers' theme
Was meant my keeping, it'd seem
Sunken by the lagustream
Lancelot why Esperance?
A sword that has shown to ally
So discrete, a deft touch too shy,
Long sleep thy keeper, has to try,
It inwardly chants. 3

And from longing which to falter
Didst encourage change to alter
Leaves, they say an only daughter
Yearning waits a man who'll court her.
In cower to Esperance
To show the while however waiting,
Wouldn't harm than harass baiting,
Misery, followed by this slating.
Extends to these chants. 4

Part II
Where shalt keep this heart of trust?
To stanchion him, above all must
Keep whispers low, from hearing, just!
As though to sprinkle word like dust
Tragically, Esperance.
Shows I am weak, thy strength to seek,
Would send ye down where all is bleak
It merely overthrows unique
Exclaim attunes to chants. 5

And from the breeze it brings coerce,
Remind us truths, a fateful worse,
Mentioned that I would disperse.
Such as said the so-called curse;
Darkened by Esperance:
Swoon would gather of the shade
They'll come as surely to parade,
Their souls in truth a story swayed
By listening to chants. 6

Away from fear wore lovely trees,
'Tis Lancelot who further sees
Towards me fanning like the breeze,
It hints that futures would appease,
Drawn towards envies Esperance
If Camelot adorns a bright,

As would a water's edge delight.
Currents put the ripples right,
Glimmers some further chants. 7

Frail as waif herself turns around,
The fall on weaving pathways bound
By fervent sway and what I've found,
Are warnings with a softer sound
It makes Devil's chords Esperance;
Seem like the shrill is overheard,
Loved blindly by wanders blurred
With what is left of meadows stirred
Angst slurry calls the chants. 8

Part III
With tall grass shaped the Typha bide [Cat-tail plants]
Along ways fetch do clothe thy side
Prepares its banks with wholesome pride,
To breach the tare at one end tied,
Invite my Esperance;
Willows token to see thee wed
Thou journey's gown did outlay spread.
As vastly smells where I have tread.
Grasping heaving chants. 9

Like dragging freely forming air,
The lift it brings to take me there
Cannot beholden solitaire
To trudge a frantic morning prayer,
Expected from Esperance:
Makings of grandeur appear host,
That besides broken hearted most
Will ail thee woe half happy toast,
Eerie solemn chants. 10

Bent in ways smoothed by how lowly
Weak-willed is, what dredge lifts wholly
Helped towards – gain a pelmet slowly

With boat in swathe soft guacamole,
A mere look, a forged Esperance,
Art to close the eyes like never felt,
Before like wary, seething svelte
It deludes debauchery, feelings melt,
With water rustling chants. **11**
And where to steer thy onward fate,
Would untie first, leave lone to spate;
Somewhere to hither leading straight,
Unto Camelot loves long wait!
Long enough into Esperance.
Can cease to look let alone spoor
A heartbeat murmur could endure,
"Venit Tempus", thy insecure.
Vacant chants. **12**

Where love, are you, that love shall find;
Where seek'd is love, shall know if kind?
Where for art thou if love is blind?
Where before I'm heard, if the mind,
Asked to be Esperance.
The ill wind calling thee, cannot,
Keep thy memory Lancelot,
Sir, I insist, where I'm brought.
There are no chants **13**

Part IV
With a somewhat ill feeling queer,
Her passing over as was near,
Where her lover is, what is clear
Suspicion doesn't arouse fear!
She'd looked towards Esperance:
To see if waiting, Lancelot,
Was where he said, to tie the knot,
The rope the boat his hands had got!
Their love tied to the chants. **14**
Her boat's arrival had first sworn –
To seeing that believed she'd warn

Speaking of the scene stillborn,
A knight enamoured, face withdrawn,
Resemblance of Esperance:
Lancelot then closing in on her,
He'd mutter to the point, a blur
"Death be commoner to deter!"
Muffling the chants. **15**

Woman, how come solemn chase
Hast carried since with limp embrace?
My fear's upon reproach your grace –
I hadn't realised death for trace,
The same as Esperance;
I thought was far, from whence you came, [**Guinevere**]
Then Lancelot, 'tis not your blame,
A knight to perpetrate the name.
Her gallantry chants. **16**

1 – She has become pale and yearnings are more a waste of time
2 – If Lancelot doesn't come to me, I shall go to him
3 – She explains the sword in as much as she is, by his side
4 – Word of gossip and hesitant decision making to go.
5 – Prepares to do something about leaving Shalott
6 – a prophetic statement, the breeze whispers it to her
7 – breeze differentially can speak of love as well
8 – She is weak but persists in making the journey
9 – Describing the scene and the walk to the river side
10 – Typha, cattail plants at the river side
11 – Explains how she got into the boat
12 – Too weak, she sets boat to set its own course
13 – In her delirium, she mumbles
14 – Her last words
15 – Narration to her end, with introduction to Lancelot
16 – Lancelot confides to his queen a final message
Footnotes: Esperance – obsolete, or in these works, the state of mind.

SPECIAL

DEDICATIONS

A

SPECIAL

DEVOTION

Brother Ray, never did you make any complications for anyone, at any time. Your innocence was surely blessed, I am so proud of you. So much so, I was inspired by John Keats for having written for his brother George that an incentive, to write one just for you. Inspired by a poem by Keats, titled, "To My Brother George",

To My Brother Ray – Bibliographic Record

Consort the many years tho' light the breeze
That you Ray, have kept more than a fair share
Like, before you were born; the shrubland air
A keepsake Fabaceae filled with colourful trees, --
And neither was our woodland lair to seize
At each crossroads, a glade our lives compare, --
How change seemed delirious, to prepare,
The life and times for which our own did lease.
O'er time Ray, it's not been far from said,
Survival with this evil patois one chooses
To disdain, the half-truths the gossips spread
They start a chain reaction which excuses;
You my brother, you're without blame or fault,
That pride be working class for common salt.

Ray spent his last days at the Villa Maria Private Nursing Home, July, August 2020. His comfort was very much on the minds of the nurses and carers. For over 40 years the focus of the home, it need not change, since there is exceptional atmosphere there, which tells you, the solemn promise I felt by the actions of the staff there.

Delivering a service overwhelmingly high in standard, the name 'Villa Maria', must stand out like a beacon, the quality of life shall sustain until sadly, one is no more. The dignity of making the needy much loved, it has instilled a faith in me that will remain forever, knowing a place exists, angelic and kind to have me classify it heavenly, during this time at the Villa Maria.

Therefore, much of the love and care which Ray had in his life, came from the brilliant caring staff and nurses at the Villa Maria Care Home, South Croydon. His last days must have been endearing to say the least, to make him feel more comfortable. Many thanks go to Juliet and Debbie for their support.

Whatever the hardship, it is over and beyond the call which speaks of a body of people or even individuals, who affect you in ways it is so difficult to describe. Exceptional feats indeed, that dedications are very much anticipated as noble. The unsung heroes whose actions speak for themselves. Forget about the poetry for a moment, while it hasn't sunk in yet, fittingly, and unrelated to cancer, that certain individuals must be mentioned.

Many of the poets I know have been friends with me for over ten years, but what makes them extra special is, they remain constant in their rising as the dawn does, anticipate, their willingness to rise another day.

MY BROTHER, [18TH August 1958 – 1st August 2020] Letter to My Brother Ray

Many kids who lived in and around The Glade & Mardell Road, Croydon, Long Lane woods at that time, [1966], played there. Collecting dead wood as well which went towards making a super bonfire on Guy Fawkes night. "Parting Through a Shade" was written as a reminder of our childhood.

Parting Through a Shade

Walks engage serenely thoughtful wood,
How eloquent, - for nature stoops below
Where shade is found to mean, forbidden tho',
I'll search, if not allowed, that's understood.
I can but recognise some mellowed fern,
Below me, as I stepped to find my way…
So innocent, what pleasant finds I yearn?
To reach the mental aspect doves display.
While lost, so swift a find, the once refrain,
The object of the walk, whilst diligent,
Abstain, while still as children, oh we feign,
To dream, our paths to cross the long intent.
I do remember gladly how we played
You'll recognise how many paths pervade.

Philippians 4:13.

"I can do all this through him who gives me strength"-

"I carried on regardless, words you did not want to hear. Then I shall honour your request... they shall be written.   --- Tony

THE LOVE YOU ARE NOW RECEIVING

IS GREATER THAN ANY LOVE BEFORE

MAY YOU REST IN PEACE RAY

MY MOTHER, [24ᵗʰ August 1931 – 31ˢᵗ December 1980]
Housewife, and Head Cook

Dedicated to my Mother, Joan Margaret Harrigan who died of lung cancer, admittedly, chain smoking would not have helped. Rest in peace mum. 'Significant Weary' speaks of Whistler's mother, and I feel it is befitting of you also mum.

Significant Weary

Impatience and pursed lips show reluctance
remaining upright, unwilling the mother;
thin – withdrawn, without further utterance
to have hurried me along, for rather...
she, insisting with the conscious overbear,
my hanging on, brief movements would disdain
through course from the preamble, full on glare
a shadow with disorder shown mundane,
which happens to be dark, from grey, a stark
divide, love's lapse and the insipid show
of surplus, which brought together, only dark!
The vacant signs through listening bestow.

Belonging to and both, separated amongst,
the recovery, since it is that ochre is an anchor,
which reluctance sits upon, mother angst
many, who'd they'd have called a canker.
Painting an incurable show of something hid,
forgives what there is to forget about fraught,
which dropped from the walls, as it partly did,
with arsenic to absorb such plight, did aught.
To distinguish from change, in kind to reason
discovery which was mentioned, more a query
gathered, we are as much in a winter season,
her death's portrayal shows significant weary.

Sadly, Looking Stone

From canvas to the grave shall all be still,
Let boredom seek to dwelling on all strife
That soon appeared unkempt the woeful will,
Stood riddled with anxiety through life,
No matter how long lived; she was a wife.

She'd barely opened eyes upon me now,
I leave the remnants filled with the control,
To stand there head up high and let allow,
My conscience shows this memory of how,
Proposals at the time become avow!

A darkness came from where we met to this,
And loss became my dignity thus moaned,
Remorseful by appearance, though I miss
The madness her indifference had owned,
By right, the omen sadly looking stone!

Where pitiful reluctance shall consume,
Disturbance of the mind has left for dead,
Already clearly shown, a quiet gloom,
Dependent is the conscience I've instead,
Relied upon the illness of widespread.

Fate had somehow closed the books on an unborn child,
[January 1950]. Before I came into this world. My mother was
coming to terms with a miscarriage, and a son she would have
had. I can only imagine what any mother goes though. I was told
this tale by my father, only once, that it had played on her mind
for over year. I could not forget a brother without leaving a
dedication for him. The abbreviation Q.E.D. was found from
the 17th century, as a stamp of authority which says, "I'll prove
what I set out to do."

To the unborn brother who I never came to know

Q.E.D. [Quod erat demonstrandum]

matris conscientiam,

For whom it was a better world a womb opposing stature.
Presents us with this, an afterlife existence, of the world,
To exude primitive form, as anathema, or Mother nature,
'Twill include fearless aesthete, it's purposed art unfurled.

 Solace, the aphotic state to exclude a violaceous moment,
When senectitude has risen, it's sadly when its cataclysm;
Becomes mute, as yet, astute to memory, time is exponent,
To the diatom, Lucida, its distance will outshine paroxysm.

Outside of what unfeeling brings we can conserve lament
Sadly, not to listen, tho' since logophobia will find a death,
Forbidden becomes enclosed on who's unaffected, I resent
To inform you, an aftertaste of saccharine, it is shibboleth.

Do not forget, this chimerical world, it is, - a painful one,
Fragility is frequent, to rosette each scintilla, as the toxoid
Seems to create panacea, away from melancholia, to shun
The Nemesis, will become ever present, and will not avoid.

Heartsease forgives the larger picture when you are kinder,
To light the world, a world you once forgot to bring me in
Mescalin the moment, briefly, you will see I did not hinder
The last goodbye reminder, one who hears, we find herein.

To you brother, had you survived, you would have been named.
Such was this misfortune mine, not to have known you, I can
assure you, 1. We would have been close, and 2. We would have
taught each other, and 3. I truly feel we would have never been
alone.

MY FATHER, [8ᵗʰ April 1927 – 6ᵗʰ March 2007]

Scrap Metal, then Foundry Foreman

Dedicated to my father Alfred Joseph Smith who was a proud man, and a very strong man, gifted with muscles. Although a man's man, it may have been expected that manliness was everything, whereas I am very much a romantic and a life-long supporter of the woman's rights. I am in every way a passionate man whereas my father was just a plain sweet man.

To feed and clothe your child and to be a loyal provider, was very much a way of life. But up against it, my father chewed the bit, and as the eldest sibling, it seems the pressure of a family of six, meant that my father worked very long hours. Meanwhile, my mother's irritability would be blamed for having just, 'a bad temper', when in fact instead, an underlying medical condition would cause her mush distress, and to the family as a whole, I sensed my father would find difficulty coping, that all my mother had done was cook and look after us but we children knew and she is very much missed. A father and each of his four children would mourn differently over our mother. It may have taught my father how to cry, no matter how strong he was.

Universal Measure
Atlas: **From the 'Pillar of Hercules**, quantum

Upon the seat which heralds the pillar of Hercules,
My captive time would confer to find the unknown;
A network of ideas which tends complexity as rules
What common-sense decides on, things more prone.
To transfer the rescue of the mind, to keep it sound
Replenishing appeal, to reform, exchange is found.

My wish to judge what is an impediment, and found
Far to be my scape, it seems I'd remember Hercules
For his strength to uplift the spirit, listen to a sound
Portray all things like they flock in what's unknown
The clouds array the conditions somewhat prone,
To impart randomly, a door opens here, favour rules.

I do not listen twice, the distinguish chance it rules
One's fate it is to plant, suspicious clouds are found
Like wishful thinking to judge unwisely, I'm prone
Beneficiary to this world of nature, unlike Hercules,
His physicality is mercy to the gods those unknown
Derivatives, like the few unseen, the apparent sound.

Whose yearn can infiltrate human error then sound?
Unduly since inconsistent bias, optimises most rules,
Unending work are these needs of ours with it found,
That nature holds us bound by this strength unknown.
Universally, I trust you'll hold this further Hercules?
Impending thwart against one's wish I hope is prone.

High above where mind inverts, we're merely prone;
Nature's omnidirectional approach exceeds to sound
Unsuspecting fear, thus it is whilst boldly, Hercules,
Illustrates the human weakness of creating the rules,
Beyond the hopes and dreams, they're all unknown
As I remember, 'time the intense', an age is found.

Death merely relates to nothingness, what is found
From nothingness, includes all vacant space, prone,
Erstwhile, to keep within a means of this unknown
Equation, all fully coherent to the frequency sound,
Unable is to arbitrate further than to bend the rules,
With this thought on weight, it is nothing Hercules.

Fear is an unknown, prone as the thoughts of sound,
We hear, but until the rules of a relatively unknown
I'll clear the void for an itinerant such as you Hercules.

It was not the fault of my parents for the lack of love, since WWII had disrupted their own childhood and young adult age during that dreadful time between 1939-45. My mother was only 8 years of age and my father, merely 12. To blame them for the lack of love or insensitivity, maybe it was an unfortunate time to have been born at all in the 50's. I did have at least my favourite grandfather and his love was tactful, pleasant natured, gentle and warm.

William, Victor Harrigan, [1889 – 1962]

With Posthumous Thanks

Survival they say is a proud thing, I trust you are listening;
I was young, too young to appreciate you more, if thanks
was loyalty, it was my loyalty to you which proved often
thoughtful, any thanks for showing what seems forgotten,
misunderstanding love relived your pain, 'twas very much
that love from me sustained to envisage such pain without.

To save you from the problems back at home, it's without
life's blessing, 'that was me', you said, as constant listening
devout and true thanks from what I've learnt so very much
it is often regarded to openly suggest the smile if for thanks
received, the order in which these names are not forgotten,
the silence is theirs, listening to things which haven't often.

Perhaps hiding, or looking out, or overlooking, more often than not, I have succeeded to evaluate many years without you in my life you made me who I am, you aren't forgotten it's with much pain to say, you were the only one listening, I have laboured ever since to find what love is, with thanks you receive, it is done I feel to win your trust, just as much.

I have a purpose in life to be without, and there isn't much to offer that I've not been spoilt, in any way, parents often struggle, I'd noticed differences pending with given thanks to those who accept being poor, as normally going without, it's very much in hope of generosity it meant little listening that the other side had landed, that war was soon forgotten.

I do compel eagerly pursued by sadness, the life forgotten, since perhaps we're wealthier than most, Britain is as much the ally, making amends for what it didn't do then, listening with an understanding means to share you so much as often, as we can it's with your granddad I'll succumb wait without, fate interrupting the good times, grieving done, with thanks.

Beyond the war you succeed to bail me out, it is with thanks consider your survival my own fate, it must not be forgotten that I survive as well that parents then were as much without forgetting who their children were, to come to say how much they suffered too, it's in a way to say thanks, if late it is often said of late that whilst we wait for always God stays listening.

Grandad, you are not forgotten, those you sought with much, affection, there wasn't often time to say, they fought without fear, or ask for thanks extending trust as a welcome listening.

The crucial element of friendship, it was never letting on when our eyes first met, how strong a love it was. Miss Maureen Dunkley would become that elusive dream. And 'all good things do come to those who wait' they say. Well? It was a lengthy one, 29 years and 61 days it took for that reality. Maureen became Mrs Maureen Smith, on the 5th September 2015, - it was a dream come true. And yes, it would include a few ups and down along the way which strengthened our resolve.

A long-distance relationship took place innocently at first, until friendship took its next important step into a remarkable starry-eyed, and romantic journey, via the pen of course. It was to keep my own sanity, for we were apart many years in total. To deal with virtually locking myself away. The intensity of love was all mine for love had not flourished Maureen's side, but being consistent in my finding the perfect woman, it seems she was as elusive as ever. Maybe it was God's idea to place the impossible position of misery, but would my prayers be answered? The more I go back to our meeting the more it makes sense. That timing had angled our movements that day, Saturday 29th November 1986. Had Maureen decided to go to church on the Sunday, or had my brother brought food home that night after decorating his lounge, I would not have been hungry that night to find in the corner a sweet angelic thing, God's will was to bring to the table the sweetest of angels.

Our Courtship – Sonnet Crown

i.

Far from wanton, dejected by this time
What force of nature was at hand that day?
To steal the pure of heart, if it be crime?
Fate ushers in the silent witness, trey. –
Some of the most, unlikeliest places,
Treasures are found, fondly not forbidden,
Longing has begotten since, tiny traces,
Tourmaline her eyes indeed have hidden.
Gusto has so enlivened me, this invite,
The tiny corner love opens wider
Her eyes begin to smile in ways moonlight,
Shines, but how much could there be inside her?
Love has spoken in ways silence deters,
Not to speak of love, caring she prefers.

ii.

Caring has a worldly good with faith to show,
More precious within, this love it forbids
The sake of 'love', the word, to wilt, Hell no!
Truths are perhaps so right to close those lids.
Time the healer, appeals to one's nature,
Labour, as the arduous task maker,
Encouraged to serve the love, by stature,
Time will tell, should ours become the taker.
To speak the truth in hindsight, remedy,
That not so handsome men have the appeals,
We in depth, have got along splendidly,
Sincerely felt is what true love conceals.
The depth of luxury between good friends,
In fairy-tales this where love transcends?

iii.

In chaste were we, it had never mattered,
The latent expiry between friends ensued;
As for a good cause the dreams it shattered,
With mind agape, more distance was pursued?
For the good reason, why tho' forest dale,
Have I to twain encumber with this drone?
That in your furthest mindset shall prevail,
Your luck was once a love, it was on loan.
If should you on a bright day find a ridge,
Then uppermost for which against the grain
You'd addle on over to Woodside Bridge,
Whereby a second chance shall ease refrain.
From whence I came, it was I dearly roam,
A fetch from not so far, near to your home.

iv.

I've kept on a torn piece of pink paper,
Her address in India, the first time we met,
Mussoorie one's place, in case we taper,
Furthermore, it sways towards the sunset.
Bestowed to faith the love of a mother,
Whose only daughter serves as a betroth
Try, keep the rain from falling, come over,
While tears on parting leave a trace to both.
It's in the furthest sense, I am not safe
Six weeks is merciful two years, like death…,
I am reminded to hold onto faith,
The time it takes to find one's final breath.
Patience alone stirs the brunt of a wait,
Without her, cannot further hesitate.

v.
The letter

Without further notice, what I've written,
Added unto these letters, worse for wear
Like I, who has weakened lately, smitten,
Still, my lasting thoughts are with you, to share.
The day you left, 'twas the second parting,
Begins the book about the far reaches,
Epic nature, though love, it's still smarting
On the face of it, nothing it breaches.
About a goddess on whose chariot,
She is sat, and across the sky, she flies
It is I who holds this lariat,
To lure in forever there, air denies.
It is you, more a nymph feeling, so small,
I would have answered had you called at all.

vi.

Least expected it was my father called,
"She is here", he said, stalling had failed
"It can't be true", I said, it struck a chord
Ironing among the many clothes, detailed
A welcome thought, my father on his way
For reasons unbeknown to me she'd ask
And falsely both denying this someday,
The way my love arrived to lift my mask.
A smile from cheek to cheek it will endure,
The constant love between a couple who
Have distance and a view, which I am sure
Is she would not deceive me, she the dew?
Bright sunny mornings greet her arrival,
The sun whose rise did keep loves revival.

vi.

Constant as the days are long, the shortfall,
Beckons before setting off our last night
Together, brightens the full moon, thus all,
But once in a blue moon, there's an invite.
I still cherish the moment when she said,
Mum, wants to meet you, over and beyond
Anywhere I've been, yes, paradise I'm led,
To believe in angels, - faith, will respond.
Together, we have reached the dizzy heights,
Only clouds could be seen, I simply gazed,
Into the atmosphere where there are lights,
I've travelled long and hard, to be amazed.
Delhi with its Devilled heat should be waved,
It glows we know in her; God having saved.

For my wife Maureen, a thank you from the bottom of my heart for bringing the poet out of me and many of the thoughts within this book. In loving remembrance for all our loved ones, we shall remember them. And Maureen's mother also, who sadly passed, in 2002, to say we miss you, Mrs Patricia Dunkley, with the kindest heart you have become the epitome of motherhood, for Maureen is just as sweet and a God-fearing to speak of a mother, fondly remembered, our hearts are filled with this beautiful memory of her.

SOME HEALING FOR MY FRIENDS

Four poetry friends who are very much like family, Josie, Debbie, Judy and Rexanne. You have all had some very difficult times of late. This is just to let you know that you are in our thoughts, and are loved so very much, to think our friendships have lasted for well over a decade now.   **Love, Maureen & Tony**

Josephine, you could say the ups and downs do make us what we are, and having hardened like the hidden ores, what lies beneath can for unknown reason, reveal a kind, caring, loving human being. In some way it seems we all came from the same cut of cloth. Love is unmistakably close, but there are variants to which being loved like family can feel. You Josie, you are a romantic poet whose ability with words has blossomed. One need only read your words. We are so very much alike, if like twins, it seems our two hemispheres has linked us through a time tunnel, to say the privilege is mine knowing you.

Josephine Vella

Perhaps, poetry has helped us smooth
Overwhelming anxiety, define expression
Each to their own, and yet… depression
Tends to lead us near, as a result to soothe;
Replacing these woes beyond one's control
Yet we'll find something for your wait
It's long, but for the longest wait, it stole.
No one cares you thought I would hesitate
To bear the brunt of this autonomy, ---
Hell bent on encouraging ourselves first,
Every day would seem the same, I foresee
Bringing back the smile, being well versed
Like you are, this attraction you've within,
Obliges our eyes, love's movement assures
Others, who in adoration of you, will begin
Defining one's attention, this love of yours.

To Debbie Altiparmakis, who was on her own after her husband Pete died, I'd been a friend of Debbie's long before that episode, and so, was very surprised there was no word from her for months. Finally, she had got in touch after initiating a move so very far from where she lived before. You Debbie have amazed me with your poetry, and should you return to the poetic scene, then keep romancing.

Debbie Altiparmakis

Deity preserver, most notable kind for guidance
Endeavour is to let me remind you, mother of all,
Mnemosyne will not forget to feel, loves radiance
Enough, the pasture, to which we all become tall.
Through following, time of well-being, to those
Each of their own desires, have infiltrated thine, -
Ruminate a prosthetic wish to proclaim we chose.

Didrachme, if on whose coin this love was struck,
Embellish to pay the deeds to love its vast fortune
Becoming benefactor, glorified is what runs amok
Bilateral thinking is a two-sided coin, as the moon;
I would welcome the day hidden for one's kindness
Endear soon to speculate Demeter, a faith goddess.

Absence I have given yet to wallow in myself pity
Leaves nothing to imagine than above undeniably
Traipsed among its lost ravishes, our loveless city
Inspired by dark, it has heightened as unjustifiably
Punished are the fields and where time stands still,
As you arrived, this garnish of love's contentment
Roams the valley, enticing a display of forage will
Marinate emotion to the lost prejudices, a comfort
Admirable to the luxury of wit to further announce
Kinetic theory of love's movement being concrete,
A wanton fact, not mystery, I enviably pronounce.

Judy Carolyn Roberts, [for you and your beloved Shane]

Joyous an occasion to rectify the gift of friendship,
Utopia this place where currency is the given love,
Directly to the heart, the part where verdant nature;
Youthful it brings the soul to explain how ideally,
Convincing his woman, how long ago finds deeply,
Aligned, by breathing out, a song to think belonging.

Rightly so how an adorable existence of belonging
Ornate to angels, who'd let us encourage friendship
Learn to seek caress like lovers who ever so deeply,
Yet without this appearance, close proximity a love
Nuptial, let the heart explain the elusive call ideally
Recapturing the kindness, she the closest to nature,

Often reminisced who exhibit themselves to nature.
Beautiful, upon a free movement, is one belonging
Emit an affection, this adornment caressing ideally,
Reigns in the utmost within the ideals of friendship
Tantamount the eyes in ways, do respect their love,
Surely the last sighting your affections imply deeply.

Biased the few who have acquired to wait so deeply,
Exquisite thoughts, held yet unknown with nature,
Convince me what is seen, are the miracles of love
Augment themselves as angels, a woo to belonging,
Maybe our two different kinds we find in friendship
Equally adjust, swiftly to compare, are found ideally

Term the phrase, "I love you, this we trust ideally: -
Half-way between believing or not, angels do deeply
Exhibit a love at length, but to wait is in friendship,
Painstaking, I find patience has built up this nature
Overheard with angels, who do share all belonging
Equivocal enough, to play their part declare a love.

Tonight, for those who have encouraged us to love.
Jostle by all accounts upon the onset, above ideally,
Assertive, if not to lose the part of love's belonging,
Listen to the birds, the beautiful song is sung deeply
Administered by two, and daily do I feel like nature.
Longing for my heart to share our lovely friendship.

Blessed for this occasion, and ideally placed is love,
An angel's gift of friendship is one of course ideally
Displayed, it belongs to the spiritual being of nature.

Sadly, Judy Carolyn Roberts had to contend with the death of her son
Shane for 25 years. She published a book, "Whispers in the Wind",
dedicated to Shane, but sadly, a week before the book came to press, her
husband Maurice passed away. Therefore, this double shock for Judy, the
book finds a special place for both Maurice and Shane. I am so pleased
that Judy got some healing from that book. For she was steadily getting
worse, I had to do something drastically for her, and so, I compiled her
best poetic works to get her started. Had the idea not to publish come
about, I dread to think what would have come of Judy, who was very ill
already. I am pleased to say there has been much improvement and
recovery of late.

Rexanne Endicott

Rexanne is what I call an unsung hero, while needing help
herself, it is helping her family regardless that makes her literally
an 'Earth Angel".

On Fragile Wings

Orseis, where both of us in passing,
None would have suspected from the kind,
Fragmentations who, from goodness passing
Rightly had we stopped to speak our mind
And not to have forgot that what we'd find
Gives such a lot of joy by such discrete.
It is admirably an etiquette of care,
Let us not so over dramatize the greet,
Each has but let one know when nice is there.
Whereas 'twas blindly dealt that why instead,
It is the words you write, the kind of peace
Not knowing who you are, but what you said,
Gift wise said few reminders on release
Sophisticating ways she has compromised!

Of wings there lifts a virtue where the moon,
No weight at all can lift your once immune,
For freedom has been blessed as the reserve,
Remaining of durations of these lifts,
A freedom of the openness which gifts
Great onus on the impetus hors d'oeuvre
Intention as the best preludes as such,
let wings of nature spree their vast outlay
Entwined with one another like today,
What is it that the butterfly does next?
Negotiating flowered plants and mates,
Glides amorously close and procreates
Survival trends which change a written text.

MONOLOGUE

I cannot imagine how many of you have suffered the antagonising wait for a love one or friend to enter remission, or indeed fail in their plight. The avenues we take, because 'such and such' took place, it often shapes where we are going in life. It is into the care frame which we see often, and how they cope and care and communicate with our loved ones is truly remarkable, and often this is done without too much fuss. What amazes me more is what invigorates us to want to help, as best as we can one cannot do enough. Many of us will have this inclination to want to help, but let me tell you, 'wanting to do' is kept that way. By what I've seen, these kinds of people are not just trained, they have actually been very much caring all their lives. It is virtually impossible to find any ordinary living soul with a continuing relentlessness to carry on. They emerge to deliver the cause, like angels, and that is no exaggeration. It is caring beyond any reach of the imagination.

What I have witnessed from the nurses from St. Christopher's, is their care goes beyond what is expected and what nurse Mary had done to go out and visit my brother, plus the carers and administration staff who went beyond the call of duty, to ease our own suffering as well, and for that I salute you all. There are many out there who are unaffected and so unaware that such kindness exists. It must be instilled in our schools at what goes on behind the scenes in specialist care homes. Because if they don't, then our children will be selfish and uncaring like we have never seen before.

@tugcegungormezler

Binding Covenant

As friends we share this love of conversation,
Taken to heart, we part share our differences,
Between us, faith the sincere feeling of elation
Understanding who we are absorb preferences.
Referred to at last it becomes more a religion.
We take on board the peace and feel just safe,
In the hands of change shall it be a smidgeon,
Small amounts are considered so more a faith...

We are mutually encouraged to persevere with
Change, to think first before anyone has spoken,
It's brought together God's variant, we shall live
Under the same roof we ourselves have awoken,
To the new day, surely believing in this compline
The signs of hope are to include so many others,
It is fair to say, that privilege be mine, to define; --
The true meaning of God Himself one uncovers.

How could I not forget my friends, to leave you all a poem?
"Binding Covenant" is a poem for those going through the stages
of treatment alone, otherwise the strength of these words it is
hoped will help you be comforted at least. I sincerely hope reading
this book will keep an active mind, and that it will shorten the
wait. The strength in numbers puts us in a positive mindset, so,
don't feel alone. I am here sharing my love with you. My gift to
you is having something to read throughout your wait, and take it
from me, I know what long waits feel like, especially when we
need to divert our attentions.

My Love to you All.
Anthony Smith, [Titus Llewellyn]

Quote from Carl, 'Wayne' Jent's "Rise for Titus"

He rules as the eldest of his clan
the challenge won by conquer of feats
his name to be honoured by each man
and laid along-side the praise of Keats

Held as doctor of economist
philosopher and educator
revolutionary socialist
educated life worth living for

Be not worthy to cast out his praise
yearning only be granted vision
to understand his shared gifted ways
my life fulfilled with praise of mission…

It is true what 'Wayne' says, a man of distinction, who is
not only humble but a doctor, an economist, no doubt, a
philosopher, an educator, as it has been proved, and for
him being socially aloof, well… the living proof of that has
now been rectified.

Compiler, Charles Cuthbertson

To my learned & trusted friends,

Anthony V. S. Smith

My trip to India to be with my love, it was a romantic epic journey, [1989], it would allow myself to reach the absolute lowest point on my return, back to London, travelling alone. A defining moment that the material in my possession, and unrefined, it just needed to be put to paper accurately.

I had been advised by a work colleague, Sheila Nasir, at Ingram High, to write about the obvious dilemma it was becoming, while at the time, the standard of English I was presenting was looking pretty awful compared to that from my school days. And so, it is thanks to Maureen, my now wife for keeping me waiting, for had she not, I would have had no reason to write. It also allowed me to enter the poetical arena, and be taught over time, [17 years], the beautiful art of poetry and prose.

Going further back to 1988, philosophy across the board was studied, History, The Classics, Physics and Astronomy, all achieved high marks. Since I do have this relentless nature to learn I guess my compulsiveness would lead no doubt, at all to intercept. As I shall carry on regardless of what there is to learn. Having now become a scholar, henceforth, a debt of gratitude via the following dedications.

DEDICATIONS

Titus Lucretius Carus

Titus – His Enigmatic Verse

Now triumphant, by what you've added, Titus;
if defined to exclaim sanctify of what detritus
tormenting him means he'd write with politeness,
ushered by arousal with what it becomes, thus
sophisticated, if not to explain it as effectuous.

To believe eccentricity has a liability to discuss
his own despise as conversely, how superfluous
enough nature, he's called his enigmatic verse;

Portraying life he feels without the conscious
omens, depicting soul worthy, such for notice,
ending, with what is found from that analysis;
transcends the theory, him being superstitious.

Literature is bound by no limit whatsoever; -
Universal thought has extended yonder mind,
Creating life, death will come a time to never
Reinstate the past again, soul search will find,
Eternal, all hopes are within a means to lithe,
To consider time travel, no more intertwined
Inseparable as willing than to cooperate with.
Undermining situations free from any, signed,
Suggests the first are foremost to endeavour.

Publius Vergilius Maro, [Virgil]

Resemblances to Virgil were his schoolmates who considered Virgil extremely shy and reserved, according to Servius, he was nicknamed "Parthenias" or "maiden" because of his social aloofness. It had affected me the same until my 21st year.

Prodigium

Prodigy, what can be done with his brilliant kind?
That none can do without, it is any wonder why.
Without tutorage, all by himself, begat such find
In understanding, aligns the affirmative arbitrary
Quotas, unwritten rule seems, state has designed
Its likeness, unknown to whom it should so belie.
Or reason with, or just thoughts they are inclined
Working out if what should not fail, twould apply?
Rationale is in readiness to relate and let's remind
Ourselves, what options therefore submit as wary,
Likeness to what it affirms whilst we are not blind,
Unnecessary likeness, is the agreement we do vary.

ii.

If to eulogize hearsay, then by the name of err,
One could pass on to the next, a probable name,
Before anonymously reading my works of fame,
For an acquiring mind to expect for certain were.
Is it not heresy of reform, that defamatory word?
The tiny whispers it brings with no end of shame
This date of birth, he and I who replicate the same,
Had Marlow stirred this aghast for, as an absurd!
Yet this style of fault, known only as an atheist,
Some five hundred years ago, midst, to this day
Having lived his name with an apperceiving say,
Shall words conceive of mine that his subsist?

John Keats

John Keats and I had similar backgrounds in youth, that his works were not well understood, and only gained the reputation after his death. It had generally been both John and George who nursed their brother Tom who was suffering from tuberculosis. There are similarities with my brother Ray's passing. What Keats had achieved in 25 years is remarkable enough to have a lasting effect on me. I have incorporated a style in which Keats would be proud.

A Sense of Feeling Afterwards

Thought jest that in my lifetime that it was
A letter would it best provoke this sway,
Sensation death would not allow a pause,
To reconsider life some further say?
It is within this letter, one's last words,
"And one, 'John Keats", Romanticism said,
To show a sense of feeling afterwards
I thought it best to show my love instead.
A solemn pledge sensation asks, 'it ought',
No fear will grieve entirely, will it, death?
It's like among so many dreams you'll sort,
Just take my last, but save my final breath.
Such is it food for thought to keep the past
'John Keats who fell asleep 'twas heard at last'.

George Gordon, Lord Byron

Among other things, Byron was born with a deformity of his leg and foot, it plagued him all his life. A plainly autobiographical allegory is seen where he is taunted by his mother. What served to aggravate the suffering imposed by his deformity was the inhumane treatment he received. Thankfully should I say, my feet were just relatively flat, and with special insoles from very young an age, the faults are now corrected.

A piece inspired by Byron,
"She Walks in Beauty"

Loves Done Roaming

Prodigious beauty bright, succeeds
  The many times I've barely dared
To speak of love, where risk exceeds
  Beyond thy notice to have shared.

Delight in seeking making pleads,
  You'll mention also that she cared,
That from such friendship, godly deeds,
  Have gone from something we prepared.

Then I have waited to occur,
  How happy now composed the sun
More worthy mentions about her
  One's days of warmth, a night begun.

That silence would endear prefer,
  Insisting, what these words have done
For less more worthy glance for her,
  Respect shall weave sincerely spun.

William Shakespeare

Shakespeare wasn't just concerned with physical health, but mental health as well. He understood that extreme levels of stress could be unhealthy, as did many Elizabethans, who had a relatively enlightened approach on the psychological observations that I have taken on.

Shakespeare also used a metrical pattern consisting of lines of unrhymed iambic pentameter, called blank verse. His plays were composed using blank verse, although there are passages in all the plays that deviate from the norm and are composed of other forms of poetry or simple prose like I have done.

A Worthy Husband Song

A worthy husband song I've sung among
As many worthless husbands you will find
I've written verse aplenty actions young,
How innocent my odes, do speak of kind?

You'll vestige my sestinas, love's good will,
Flamboyant as bouquets do spread desire,
Contentment shows a brief haiku, yet still
How epics do outweigh a lifetime squire.

And here shall duly sonneteer how frail,
A worthy husband is within this means,
Too weak but not too shallow he would fail
Her needs for love to keep the tragic scenes.

My ballads shall in depth prepare to cease
A worthy husband song, some welcome peace.

John Donne

Donne featured with his frequent dramatic, everyday speech rhythms, his tense syntax and his tough eloquence, were both a reaction against the smooth which I do favour against. His early career was marked by poetry that bore immense knowledge of English society and it was met with sharp criticism Another important theme in Donne's poetry was the idea of true religion, something that he spent much time considering and about which he often theorised.

My Stairwell to Heaven

Wrote the poet, 'who succeeds as I do', -that is a misquote.""
gloat my want for a style to exist, it will ascertain a footnote.
Showboat the past, one extraordinary poet they who devote;
promote one's name the high acclaim what this will connote.

Dote an equerry to the ministry, a huge jump o'er the moat,
capote high ranks, among poets who are not worth a groat,
dote upon rhyme, a precedence again spreads the wild oat,
coat attorney, and peremptory movement aids as anecdote.

Emote trajectory when following can turn out, a cut-throat,
demote rather late with a mere modest means it aids ignote,
  float among the clouds, like they who'll write a cheery bloat;
  troat entirely, my enthusiasm dives below what's asymptote.

In addition to the classical style which I have taken upon myself to use, I have been lucky to have found worthy candidates on the world's largest poetry stage, 'allpoetry', who rank highly among the top 3% on that site. Two mentors who are sadly no more, that I should add 2 dedications to honour their being, 1. 'Penman', [Harry William Roberts], and 2. 'Poetic-Theorem', [David Randall Hall]. Of the now, the great gifted rarity of finds continues, in the shape of Andre ben YEHU, Juddbryll and Andrew Lawson.

Andre ben YEHU

O' Masterful Magician Dignitary, Mentor

Apollo, O masterful magician, it's my delight in knowing you
Never too late to reach so greater compliment, I referred to...,
Defender of the Oracle, god of light attain thee all this truth,
Recite your harps convey, this intermediary role, you soothe,
Ephemeral, as the gifts of prophecy prolongs you an esquire.
Beyond reach of the stars, supinely do I lay, I fetch you sire,
Eloquent gaze so bright, so pure 'twould comprise, I display
Naively, my guide Andre, with sonorous sounds so heavenly,
Yet diminished free from which this epoch showed so cleverly
Endeared me to create focus on Artemis, as she will focus on,
Healing and prophecy, accompany your muse, a cithara, upon
Unduly lay, that I may ask Clio, to cross your hand, and play?

A god of many things, poetry the knowledge of art will cling,
Nothing, and I mean nothing can replace, I besiege no rivalry,
Duly, centre of the earth Delphi, with the Titan Leto quietly,
Ruminating an important remedy, each is privately speaking,
Each to their own, as they say a friendly exchange is chivalry.
Blatantly obscure, since the Greek legends have left for us,
Eons, they're sifted to placate last the redeeming lost services
Numerate each, their instruction that is through those mercies,
Yearnings are, as the Apollon Musegetes, do necessitate, thus,
Emancipating both desires, but our thoughts do freely acquire,
Hedonism, for it attributes thru' listening, learning, to inspire,
Unilaterally your fragrance lives wise on words without a fuss.

The idea of mentorship comes about with time, and having got the feel of thought from Andrew Lawson's subtle inviting comments, they say and mean a lot with a conservative amount of feedback. It is never ruthless with Andrew, always fair in comment and with his wry sense of humour. Most probably like the many poets who a fair-minded, that comments do come at a premium. They are seen to help but never hinder, while some humour among us would not go amiss.

Creating Legends - Andrew Lawson

Superbly felt, that custom made couture
Negotiates each year, the whole conform
Dressing the remains of what aids nurture,
Remnant of the classic art, a mere reform,
Encrusted, the jewel to the crown a noble
Writer, you've exceeded praise; than most;
Labyrinthine, how widely spread and global
As many thoughts my man tend to riposte
Welcome, this laureate is one possession
Soothing poets, we prepare ourselves for;
Other than you who has asked the question
No one can, I mean no one deserves it more.

A Special Mention - Michael Thomas

Michael Thomas has, in my eyes, and for a while now, been such an inspiration. His contests in those early day were a magnet for the very best poets. Take it as a mark of respect from all your fellow poets. The glorious brethren of the 'allpoetry' society, hail your ingenuity, which you sir have set examples difficult to raise. Whereby the many nations who congregate, to share your worthy status.

Juddbryll

"I was born with pen in my hand, scrolls in my head and scripts in my heart...I scribble from my soul; and deep within my depth lay fountains of lyrics, rhymes and rhythms bestowed on me to bring magic to this tragic an ever-busy realm. "Juddbryll

The statement above speaks volumes by what is tragic and an ever-busy realm, is that Judd would find precious time to put a word in for you. And a creditable poet who I have known over the years, that some time be put aside to share with others. And I say Jacobean, simply on a personal note, the Jacobean era, [1603-25], to have created harmony between the present day and taking part in intellectual complexity with this Metaphysical poet, myself.

Jacobean, you have created such harmony
Undertaken to bring philosophical stance
Dedicatory self-worth, and what company
Delights me more to cherish this alliance -
Brings the utmost respect to you my man;
Regarding stature, it is with a leading role,
You maintain dignity that the master plan
Lasting an effect your words bring, cajole,
Learning practices, this, our watering hole.

Poetic-Theorem, David Randall Hall

A very good friend and mentor who is sadly no more, and this was 1 day before his 52nd birthday. His brilliant mind as a mathematician, shone a very humble man. Insightfully he was a brilliant creator of verse and deliberating a number of solutions rather than just one. And so, it was to honour David Randall Hall with a Poetic Theorem for our very own 'Poetic-Theorem' to work out.

Poetic-Theorem

Pythagoras, I call my dearest friend
of which to be fair equals minded, and
expedient a master makers hand,
to shake it for the grandeur of depend,
in excellence astounding manners can,
consider this I'm rounding it down.

Triumphant as the banner wielding chant
helped wisely by the hailing our dear man
each spokesman more a willing penchant,
of poetry, rhyming free for tedium,
regardless of the state, the infiltrate,
enigmas which create the medium
mathematician, theorist, atomic weight.

Put up against the laws that gave its name
officialdom the martyr both proclaim,
enactment of the foe, what kindly foe,
transgresses maths to be confusions though?
in Titus could he choose a nicer woe?
content to find this master guise, hello!
-
The principles of all things culminate
hypotenuse to be attracted accrue
each angle to the volume equalled too
opposing each with equals, is my mate,
reliable and sound and twice as nice
engaging information of growth rate
my exponential friend in clear concise.

Now, if you had described saving the 'best till last', it could be credited to only one man who influenced many, to include the many battles between ourselves in Michael Thomas's contests. Because of that, your name will be best remembered as a friend, while poetry remains at the heart of my respect of you.

The Penman Wrote

N.B
1. Victorian times
2. Roman times
3. Mediaeval times
4. Modern times

1.

A penman once wrote, "it takes courage, boldness and tenacity", to which I most ardently agree, that there are various styles to consider, being stained as having modestly just wrote. There is more palatable means to contest by, be it moderate or not, - not room enough. To compare other men by, for which you are certain, can to hone the yardstick of ten paces.

2.

Had I left Roman times, none to discover myself into the deep, dark lustre of death laden, gladiatorial terms between their legions, having left signatures of blood for having written, a penman may along this route, show to be victorious, this total invasion. Envy from his fellow men, a matter of honour to which the gladiatorial term applies, he'd pen his name.

3.

I dare say, I do include the decent pluck of courage that determines the feathered quill, to write bountiful account of one's own life, contesting those who've lost their will against who endeavour to leave a name, his soul, though through the ages one's consent.

I can diligently feel obliged, on what the future holds, for this the pen has written, a matter of honour.

4.

'Penman', conqueror of the will to write the minds of men finds their stumbling the edifice, a battlement, adaptable to any capture attempt, so rightly steals away his quilled beleaguer I am one of those, whose admittance is to all conquering, yet I too am deceived being eager. Torso of the Titan, amicably so and do accept it more of a myth, when there's another known legend, the penman.

Penman commented on this piece above, 17th January 2010.

"Oh my, I'm really overwhelmed by your creation. It is so incredibly crafted and stunning in its presentation. I feel very humbled and extremely honoured by the time and thought you took to write this. Thank you for such an amazing write. Not sure I feel as deserving as you created this masterpiece, which truly reflects on your own incredible talent.

GLOSSARY

ANALYSIS, OR

JUST STATING THE OBVIOUS

GLOSSARY

General insight on the poems you've read

~Hortensia~

Hortensia, commonly named Hydrangea; The elegance to which the petals outreach, a ballet would position Venus at her birth: The backcloth wholly floral. N.B. – Decyl; noun, Chemistry. A group of isomeric univalent radicals, a group behaving as one

~A French Garden~

Feminine verse of the Hydrangeas, gossip about the privets, [Masculine], within the confines of a small space, a garden in London, then, our host compares it with an area on France, known as the Roman Brocomagus.

~By Modest Means~

Inspired by a quote by Hemingway. "Why should anybody be interested in some old man who was that failure?' Ernest Hemingway. The author takes it personally to argue the fact, about his own success.

~The Perfect Storm~

Just simply, an inspiration from the film, "The Perfect Storm", leading the reader towards that ultimate sad finale from the film. The human acceptance, so different to the poem's backlash.

~First Love, Like Still Waters~

A couple meet for the first time, they try so very carefully for fear of making ripples on the water, so ruining any chances to impress.

~Love's Exponential~

The magnification of Capella, within the Auriga Constellation. It is explained to the sweetheart, using the trajectory as a whole to see how near from so far.

~Ode to Melancholy~
Sleep is disturbed; The consistent sad or bad luck from the past, it does not give the future a chance to change for the good, with what the past has given, hence the lack of optimism.

~The Arctic & the Walrus~
A tiny metaphorical piece about the future of all animals and not just the walrus in the arctic regions, re; the mild climate. It is to have us made aware.

~One Beautiful Time Piece~
'One Beautiful Time Piece' it speaks of my wife, like many of my love poems about her. For it was Maureen Dunkley, who brought poetry into my life, although unaware at the time for me to tinker with.

~Honeysuckle~
The Honeysuckle with its eloquent scent, especially during early evenings, it's bearing down to engage we ought to assume or liaise without ought to encourage love's keeping, for which I am reminded.

~Beauty & the Beast~
There is a beautiful 'Lady & the Tramp' story interwoven within to include the 'Beauty & the Beast'. And the obvious romantic feel for 'whether or not', or, 'for always.'

~For Her, the Stone-Grey Walls~
A wealthy widow in Rome, that mournful time where only a priest dare call. The stone-grey walls lead you down the narrow street, telling us about her mind at this moment, with respect.

~Love, the Way it Is~

There are no right or wrong ways when it comes to love. It is rather hit and miss the avenues we take, to use the worth of good intent, the true gut feeling, they whether right or wrong, love will shape itself in the end.

~In One Another's Thoughts~

Narcissus comes to life with outstretched hand which tugs and the approval the lake holds. A turn from looking back to see the doves nesting, and flitting from place to place, carrying and dismantling the daffodil stems.

~Earth Assigned Ascesis~

Facts do show two lovers who each had difficult upbringings. Serendipity would bring about 3 chance meetings. Long-distances and faith would not defeat two soul mates before they could be entrusted to each other... for the good?

~Forever Autumn~

It could be said by Shakespeare to compare thee to a summer's day that autumn at this blessed time 'thou art lovelier and more temperate', that the British autumn, now the summer of old to call it my favourite season.

~Corcyra – A Sleeping Beauty~

'Kindness is kept to shape the waters around Corfu as Poseidon's search continues to calm the waters, especially when it came to some beautiful bays, [inlets], where it was hoped Corcyra could be found.

~A Pelagic Love – Corcyra & Poseidon~

The waters explain our beautiful summer holiday of 2017, to put myself in the place of Poseidon for this modern era. The small lagoons which we found in Gouvia. Cove of the romantic kind, to hide ourselves in.

~Beware the Whirling Dervishes~

Clouds play the part of the whirling Dervishes in a formal ceremony known as Sama. It is however practiced by other orders of the Muslim faith to reach religious ecstasy. Rumi, is unravelling his turban by this time, 1250, Konya, Turkey, saying, "Search beyond the clouds" –

~Hershey – Acrostic~

The Hershey Company, commonly known as Hershey's, is an American multinational company and one of the largest chocolate manufacturers in the world. Milton Hershey made his mark as a successful confectioner. He was by no means an overnight success, nor did his achievements come without the usual hardships.

~Litore Volutus – Rubaiyat~

Litore Volutus, or for another word for a beach bum, who. Bless him, is not much of a poser to have us know what he's thinking. To explain in a nut shell the insecurities of a man who may not be so cool a dude, but we can get carried away with his dreams.

~Proscenium Colonnade~

Varying shades of green are exposed, as we sail down a quiet ravine, the glorious scene is met with some pretty words. A supporting role to have us exit left, which catches the eye as did the bridge, to add a Shakespearean touch.

~My Wish for Snow, a Blur – Sonnette~

From as far back as I can remember to the 1970's, Christmas time, it would add the pleasure of snow. It was typical for its time. But now, more often than not, and sadly, snow, I think of the past.

~So Rare a Flower~
Love has nature to compare, which shows in many of my romantic works, but, for such a small poem, we must worry for a diminishing species, and so precious finds.

~A Classic Love Story~
After watching the film, "Titanic", it somehow compares with ours that yes, it was epic, but then aren't all waits? In hindsight, survival is dependant on the ups and downs we had. Unlike Jack and Rose, whose story resembles Orpheus and Eurydice, ours did not look, 'between the first, and last time my eyes opened'.

~What Beautiful Verse, Dreams Create ~
I find from a restless sleep, in the middle of the morning, when all of a sudden, vivid details from what was left of sleep, and a loving look upon my wife asleep before I write.

~A Sunny Silence~
This poem reveals the sound a field of daffodils make while bees with their begging bowls arrive to collect the nectar. It's a common thing to see, amid infrequent listening.

~Healing Power~
It doesn't really need an explanation on what holding hands means, so, when your life is dependent on what is a sense of comfort would behold. You'd be alone otherwise but for one other.

~The Quality of Friendship Your Goodness Brings~
It speaks of so few friends, but then that's what makes friendships special, by giving it a more meaningful approach. Plus, it didn't need more than 3 stanzas to explain. Any more would have ruined the feel of the poem.

~Fenestra ad Animum~
The quicksilver ease of movement the sclera fills, drawn towards the centre of the iris, there holds a confluent, soft moisture which glistens to draw two lovers in to that grand abyss.

~Our First Kiss~
Oh yes, I remember it well, one rainy night, and indeed I believe we both trembled that night, and I should say naively. There is not a person reading this who could forget, and I one rainy night.

~Papaver Somniferum – Lauren's Grape ~
Papaver Somniferum, simply put, the opium poppy with a feminine description, her purity has been lost to sapphire, or a magenta aspect. And silk to many kingdoms, queen of the blooms.

~A Gaze Given Scene~
The exploration of space travel by means of illustrating the stars that nothing is impossible. This piece comes from another book, "Earth Angels". That the sincerest intentions are those who are serious enough.

~Nymphs, Angelic Notes~
Nymphs were often a rank below the gods with an accent on presiding over natural phenomena, from the ground to the edge of the atmosphere. Angelic notes are given to spur on the free will. As courtiers or souls who wait the adornment of wings.

~Oncidium – An Orchid~

The second poem on the orchid, so highly prized and being precious, that once again, 'little was more' in terms of verse and the explanation for our 'dancing lady of delight'. 'Majestic perhaps, to conceal the orchid, any mishaps.'

~Tall and Fetching Glances~

How with our imagination of the Savannah, private thoughts forbid us to seduce a hidden shore? A scene from far away from the outreaching landscape, lions and elephants thrive. But then, look towards the palm trees.

~Beauty Besides – Acrostic~

The sad state of affairs, that a lack of confidence for some women is, to take a little advice. It is hoped a few words said in the right direction will put to right. Like in the mirror for example?

~Mermaid of Zennor~

Zennor is a place that exists in Cornwall, the story from 1873, of a mermaid, and her search for the beautiful voice. It came from the St Senara's Church, and Matthew, whose fate it was to fall in love with her. The people of Zennor, would never see him again, after he fled to the sea to find her.

~Love in the Highest – Reverse Abecedarian~

A reverse abecedarian ascends, showing the first letter of each line alphabetically. For reasons the rise to heaven is understood, the opposite can be either related to God, or the return of Christ.

~The Angel I'm Bestowed To~
A poem that is personal to me, during the most awful time, when all of a sudden, she comes into your life. It is something I am indebted. You'd bequeath anything for her. It is admirable to think by the grace of God, that some miraculous things do happen.

~Faith, How Far Away~
This poem speaks of Faith of our choosing. Whether it be within touching distance, or not at all, it should gauge the clearest conscience, and I actually keep mine within touching distance.

~Hurt for Others, Aft Yourself~
Having some concern for others who are hurting, and there are many who do automatically, and without thinking, do speaks to those with an ounce of care within.

~Love Portrayed – Cinquain Form Chain~
Cinquain is a lyrical form for which more is said with a minimum of fuss. Love is spoken of with bucolic scenes in mind, and of the spring, (birth), and whatever the future may hold.

~Antirrhinums~
The snapdragon plant is a favourite plant for many gardeners, but not everyone knows about the darker side of these plants, once the seed pods have dried out... how remarkably alike, they'd resemble skulls. The flowers themselves you'll not forget either.

~If I Could I Would~
While much of the time we are willing to help others, there is an endless scurry of needy people, who in themselves may think we do not care enough. It is to those we try but sometimes one cannot possibly help all.

~The Stoic Elk~

The woodland scene leans towards the dusk, while in among the trees a solitary hut, to hint at the oblivious nature, and out of view an elk I would imagine in deep thought.

~Love's Enchantment~

"This self-preservation" poem was written almost 30 years ago, when all I could do is dream of accomplishing a find as was the case. And yes, having alerted the future without really, much to go on. But please enjoy our beautiful love story.

~Ego Semper Admonendi – Sestina~

In short, the title is contextual for "I will always be"…, and constant. The truth of the matter, a letter I received after going no further than friendship, to take love a little bit further.

~Comparative Healing~

Having praised a woman very highly, that she would become my very own muse. I put myself into a precarious position of always putting her on that pedestal against the traits of others. Healing came by way of closing the distance and shortening the time period between us, thus rectifying the time between us, metaphorically.

~By Love's Own Choosing~

Inspired by Lord Byron's piece, "She Walks in Beauty" as it did originate from, "Pride & Prejudice" by Jane Austen, a garden scene is depicted most definitely from a time period of around 1840's, by love's own choosing, that I myself had relied on her so choosing.

How Far, How Bright a Love

My dreams and wishes had come true, by attraction, a soothing distance, a bleeding heart even, and remaining positive even though the odds were stacked against me, fate's pulling part is like sun had within its reach to conceal the secret of such a love, and no escape. From deep within, my gut feelings were telling me.

~In Everlasting Friendship~

While it is intended that we'll reach a fair innings in terms of quality of life that hopefully to remain with us until old age. For instance, the elderly gentleman who is in a tête-à-tête with his walking-stick, that death could not even separate them.

~Shall Keep a Bed of Roses~

Inspired by Proverb 6: 1-3 5, and some generous advice on the Wisdom and its workings. And the debt of course to include sin and seduction. A keep a bed of roses the untroubled times, the long hours taking a way those you haven't got time for.

~This Self-Same Pity~

A weeping willow expresses a reflection of the self in a way no one could have told you. With the drizzle running down the window, a depression somewhat answered by the excruciating agony outside. That it would fit your own misery with its own dreary outlook, or was it all in the mind?

~Where There is Hope~

This poem speaks about the work colleague who saw what long distant love was doing to me, to ask, "Why don't you write about it, it may in fact ease your pain, it may even shorten your wait. It seems, "Where There is Hope", there is a mighty fine message which only you will find. My now wife and I were married, 80 days short of 29 years of our first meeting.

~No Truer Tale, Than Ours~

No truer tale indeed. For it speaks about all of us, for good of a bad. There is a lot of truth, for what little good can come out of our lives. Then each of us has a success story, even if out limitations have been reached, and nothing more.

~Courtesy to a Passing Glance – Roundel~

A simple courtesy between a man and a woman, for the first time, your gentlemanly ways should enamour her, with a touching moment.

~On First Approach – Semitetra~

Such simplicity, on first approach a coyness about the situation that one shy couple will make. Not necessarily shy, it may be a way of the world these days, but let's say, getting to know another took a little longer than it does now, how romantic to see, as you would with the younger teens these days.

~Escalaphobia~

Simply put, it is the fear of escalators, as I am sure you'll be aware approaching one, a little hesitancy to find that first foot hold. The poem itself was from a word bank contest, to force the issue with a choice of words, such as, 'alligators', 'marmalade', 'avalanche' and 'dude-ranch' would you believe?

~Love's Impromptu~

I never came into the light until 1986, and having kept much of my innocence under cover, it seems I've been fastened, tight by the hedera, or the ivy plant, too afraid to show myself. "to contend myself, if not, to forget love around me, a world rather forgotten...."

~Girl in Mirror~

The loss of faculty or aphasia, a girl approaching puberty, then she has a lot of questions she needs to ask herself. Before a swift turn of foot comes to calling a truce with those tiny hold ups girls have. We can only hope our children will make the right advances in life to escape the unknown.

~How Time to Spring is Set ~Acrostic~

Acrostic? Just read the first letter down on each line. The prelude to describe the end of winter leads us seductively to hint at spring the promise of good things with its fertile abundance. Recovering the many tiny traces are what will inlay a vibrant bud. Now, let the change-over begin.

~Tandoor~

A specialised oven poetically describing the heat factor, and comparing it to man's idea of carnage. He fires the brick this homage the clay has kept the tradition within finding a discrete way in cooking preparations, that time in essence is something man has no time for, whether he likes it or not, time and patience are needed to confirm how well, a typical tandoori taste.

~How Virtuous the Moon Displays~

The virtue of the moon and its phases, while there is a distance between gazing up and seeing for ourselves how beautiful it is. A larger than life distance goes unchanged between the earth and the moon, that never the twain shall meet. The tides shall shunt in opposition, as of course the moods do, the seasons do the same with the clearest intention so dearly devoted.

~Flamenco Nights~

A little history with our flamenco began, it will include the fathers of its origin, the gypsies, it will take you to the kingdom where there are tsars, and 'Baile' of course which stole the romance. The reign to which stands literal in Cadiz, one cannot forget to peruse the Marruecas fine classical intention to enhance those dancing feet.

~Pro Procul – Many Moons Ago~

It is with apprehension to have written an apology, for my absence from my poetry group. And like Hale-Bopp, I would appear out of the blue. 'Pro Procul', it simply means, 'the distance'. Hidden within this piece, is for whom it is intended. While time waits for no one, then I should make good use of what time I have.

~A Luteal Phase~

The luteal phase begins after ovulation. The sword of Damocles speaks of ovulation, (unless fertilisation occurred), at this phase, the ruptured follicle closes after releasing the egg. There are increased quantities of progesterone during this time of high spirits, chemically speaking.

~The Moral Fibre~

How I love to think back to how things were. It adds a slant to, 'The good old days' by putting in a good day's work, and being honest with ourselves as well as helping others. Although many in their 60's or thereabouts, we are outnumbered by those who have not been led by these excellent examples, and knowing who your friends are, are all long gone.

~Dawn's Abundance – Terza Rima~

Based on Eos, Goddess of the Dawn, and I perhaps Tithonus, that lustrous keeper of love, the sun on rising. First light when forever it seems at the window, rising with your thoughts, and I quote, "What helps us to raise is to gain new heights. For which she'll bring, immortal feelings borne.

~Had We Not Met~

Had I not turned to see her intent did shine on me. Had she not been there at all, the night, would have me leave, to cope alone without her light. A spark you'll find that not as many people it would bring to recall such feelings. Serendipitous to think of right now, who with, "Had We Not Met", to savour such a day.

~Season of Change ~Sestina~

Beginning with my favourite season, the autumn and like the change of mood in the forest, there are pleasures to explore. How the flamboyant light has crept in through a thick forest canopy, the so-called ghost, when an apparel plays tricks with our minds.

~Bathing is Godly – Abecedarian~

An A-Z of luxurious moods are there to replace what we hope to while away. It is in essence a chant, "Ah! Bathing!", you can almost feel it can't you? The part which states, "xenial yang zygomas", which holds a phrase, "for host and guest too indulge relaxation heavenly heat and light, upon the human skull.

~A Twilight Zone~

Or else, our 'fears', I speak of 'night owls' or 'early birds', that between both the twilight zone enables a Socrates oath. Imagine if you will, such things which we truly loathe, then, come, prepare yourself a lasting peace. A vastness that is called for to empty our minds, but many do not.

~Sensing its Autumn~

"October, the gift is this sense of grandeur, and most certainly my favourite season as I've said. The leaves fall in heaps with the warm fragrance, a courage does emerge to smell through air translucent thought.

~Breathe the New Day ~Villanelle~

You are as free as a bird to do as you wish. To rise beyond reach and as far away, and as you breathe, an easiness is assured like the open plains, all straight lines are fathomless. Just breathe and you will find.

~Poets Past, a Classic Set~

Back to a time when poets old were few and far, how we can appreciate an immortal worth to mention a bygone age would set aside a classic set of poets to provide for us, what is expected. It sure must remain timeless a feel this present day.

~Recital to a Love Vouch~

A recital, like what you would find on a locket, a poem, or photograph, or even love vouches for which here lies a truly romantic tale. "To honour thee, forever...", with the truest estimate, it will confine for thee a fullness of blossom.

A Bawdry Gaze Across –

The unedifying tale of a signet, who with its mother's frown, a peer at curiosity, the strength of a signet without its mother, that 'dirty' look or bawdry gaze. There is a Shakespearean feel about it.

~The Bogey Man ~

I remember as a small child being aroused by the bogey man. Tall shadows at the curtains, but little did I know the flapping tree outside would make my skin crawl. He would lead me with this game of watch, to torment me further, he would never sleep, the dreamer in these parts, my mind it keeps.

~The Ragdoll Nymph~

And I a lonely child, would effectivly carry myself,it is not the doll but I, who much of the time, had to console himself. Yet you ragdoll, are torn between who lives and learns to keep the love of one who shares.

~Changing Moods of Nature~

An atmospheric piece which allows the stormy winds penetrate our minds to the one inanimate object it be directed at. A silver birch reflects the minds-eyes, having closed the curtains on what was last scene. The changing moods collectively are traits we have moved from outside, it appears are herein.

~Esther – What I Would Do for Them? ~

King Ahasuerus is blind to a fault, for having found Esther, a Jewish woman. A poem which reveals the fears for her people, not herself, they are admirable. What she would do for them is equal to what she would do as for her king. Reliving the story was a pleasure for me, for you all.

~Love's Spiritual Home~

Our love within these cloisters unequivocally between us as a whole, holds such worth. The example is unduly an oyster shell. That love, a tiny speck should reach epic proportion it become the cultured pearl as it has done. Love has become wholeheartedly a spiritual home.

~Life's Ritual – The Seasons~

Before the nine, there were four Muses recognised as Thelxinoē, Aoedē, Arche, and Meletē. 'Life's Ritual', is more a Museal Response, and four sonnets with an old feel of the world.

~Pluto, Love Angst~

The sadness of Pluto losing its planetary status, you can almost feel love's angst over the distance between Earth and it. To be discarded in a way unloved would feel and almost traumatised to that point of longing, from such a long distance.

~Ancestry Land – Long Time Since~

Imagine if you will a map, a small village with a few houses and maybe some spare land. 'Ancestry Land – Long Time Since', travels forward to see how things had changed. Sadly, landslides had dramatically pilfered away what good there was.

~Under Tarpaulins – Clowns~

A contest which suggests a rose, to create a poem from it. Instead the colour of the rose becomes an after scene. I was to suggest the clambering result of the big top collapsing upon the clowns underneath the tarpaulins. A marinade of colour profiles the end result

~The Awning Shone Inlaid~

The sun is out, therefore so must the awning protrude from the house. Observations are on the shadows formed from the movement of the sun and the awning shape has shone inlaid. You could imagine a little resistance, it meant not shutting all the light out.

~The Nature of Any Doubt~

A poem which lets you move about as you please, it gives you time of existence, given the time to retain the past or actually move on. It is fully discretional on what the poem says, but then, you have to use some insight. All I ask is that you let the poem change your way of thought.

~Soul of Silk~

The silkworm has given its heart and soul, the giving of itself, the silken gown to which the bride is indebted that she too should be of chaste to wear such a gown. Not to take away from the designers, but the silkworm would be better placed as the seamstress.

~My Wish for Snow, a Blur – Sonnette~

A personal story you could say, when 40 years ago Christmas was white and so to the winters cold. It a brevity of nature which the ~ UK has its affections and the sad regret that is caught in a blur, remember the snow from a long-lost past.

~Summer's Crown Bouquet~

Seven acrostic sonnets which spell the name of a flower down each of the first lines. With insight it explains metaphorically, each flower. Partially right but all in all a personification of each flower at least, to show you, the poet tried.

~Sonnets of Titus Llewellyn~
From that period of 14 years in total
"Sonnets of Longing", levelled out on many subjects

~A Summer's Wait for May~

A period between April and June exists, and with a human touch all three months, April, May and June are very much in touch with each other. The good old British wealth which is unpredictable, all three become human in a sense to work out for themselves, a probable outcome.

~The Hay Wain~

'The Hay Wain', a painting by John Constable, 1821, and a sonnet which points out the Fagales, an order of foliage, a Dirge, or 'angel of death, and an Aigrette which as a plume, it honours the artist. The sonnet speaks of the route made by the hay wain every day.

~An All-Weather Season~

By what I call the all-weather season, the British weather has been given a fair amount of criticism, but it's more of less the same, that two of the seasons befit the dismal weather, both autumn and spring. It seems they both contribute alike to being summer, and when it comes to winter? Well, it's like we've never had one.

~Patience, Virtue~

I found her sitting there, like as if I has waited all my life. God in his mercy would find us staring at statues, confined to the spot, Mary, the woman who was chosen to represent the chosen wait, that I to cam fix myself upon. His divine mercy had discovered another lost soul, the countless times I've scuppered such theories.

~Following, an Autumn Sunset~

The one sonnet which stands out to favour autumn. For it initiates a calm incentive to consider the warmth of God's blessing and to find the perfect place for prayer, the autumn feel has a deep sense of belonging to it.

~A Playful Poet Sang~

Endearingly as sweet a poem you will find. It is the playful poet, who attracts the slightest of distraction with these facts, but he acts in way to the tune daffodils make. I can imagine him now, standing in an upright posture, with his head positively proud. My guess is the daffodils were touched by his words.

~The Effort and Demand~

The demand we put on ourselves in the heavy industries, and the trust in employees to make vast efforts are now no more. The corporate training manuals of what you can and can't do? Well, I'm saddened by the fact the ethics of old cannot be applied to the present day.

~To Raise Oneself Divinely~
Consecutive poems which speak of work then yourselves. It is the self-motivation which is lacking these days, if only for some self-motivation?

~Love's Many a Splendoured Thing~
Ah! Yes! You can imagine now, overlooking Hong Kong harbour, and William Holden with Jennifer Jones in his arms. The romance of the last 50 or 60 years, could I ever elaborate such a scene again, the classic way love can be orchestrated. And Andy William's voice sound perfect for such a scene.

~When First We Met~
It speaks very much about the first and second glance, and things we do when given just seconds to react. Thoughts of losing come to mind as would a time to be immersed, it's rather 'hit and miss'.

~Soft Acquaintance~
So often with a hasty hark, it's whether we choose to listen or not. While our ears have unmistakably heard, it seems we choose what we hear. From a speaking perspective, a soft acquaintance is such and loosely illustrated as, "you haven't heard, have you?"

~Gazing Forward, Gazing Back ~
That period where autumn comes to an end for winter to take over. Some reluctance between October and December letting go. The brown, reds and auburn are definitely worth keeping.

~A Love for All Seasons~
Then, on the other hand, love brings a timelessness, while there was distance to deal with, faith has shown courageous signs that a priceless gem was worth the wait and our hopes and dreams. In fact, the only weather I recall was the year of the great hurricane, 1987. [UK]

~The World Can Wait~
A super-hero comic was inspired to have our author go out and be one. It wasn't too distant than the one in India and back, searching skies, even Kryptonite is mentioned, then chivalry would carry the heart of superhero waiting in the wings to catch his fair maiden.

~Sounds Like Angel Wings~
Literally, with mind aflutter, we can imagine the sounds angels make, in addition to the violins and sirens. "There is nowhere on this earth I'd rather be." Then, what is this telling? It is an exceptional place where you can listen to the pulling of strings.

~Love, For What it's Worth~
A sonnet for my brother speaks of what little love there was in both our lives, at very young an age. To compare the love he never had, now, with my wife, the rarest gift of all. A gaze at my brother who had always been alone, heartbroken I was, and Ray's last wish to be with his siblings, and the closest it had ever been.

~Alone Her Conscience Chose~
Of all the men, why would she want me. It is a constant pang, but I guess loyalty of all things and being there when she needed me. 'That not so handsome men she will deter', I could not compare with them yet, but our understanding of each other found a rare but precious love.

We'd Fondly Speak –
From a true story, stands the Cinderella appearance, to include the choosing of the 'slipper', for Fate, reversing the role for which I was the pauper. It did include a lengthy wait, for the love of a princess to bloom.

~Will O' the Wisp~

The atmospheric ghostly light seen by travellers at night. The 'jack o' lantern' is another term. The dull lit whispers slow in height approaching. They exceed at length on end, like we are seeing things. The Volta attaches the sewing of the thread, our fears, on what a last request would ask.

~By Effort and Demand, the Will to Live~

Before the Health and Safety laws came into existence, a one last look before that change which spoke of common sense and assessing for ourselves, like computers do now. We were made to think that our once mental agility has been taken away from us, one almost loses the will to live.

~For Worthy Salt~

The ask was to add as many shades of blue in a poem, but what I found was a metaphor, about the true and worthy salt of life. A craft at sea or the true blue for worthy salt. The tough life of kids for thirty years. From 1938-68, but one must not forget 1913-20, it would include the recovery.

~An Elving's Harp Along~

An elf takes the place of a minstrel, within the forest where sounds do play in unison. Whether it was to engage with the sounds, or to obliterate them altogether. And I am sure, an Elving's harp was not the only instrument that night.

~See-Through Cloth~

I need not have much cloth, and little modesty perhaps. It speaks of greed, over-all, not needy. While we can rest upon the laurels of decency without paying large sums of money for it is found, for those who buy in excess, they'll be a shortage of happiness

~A Star in a Million~
Put the woman of your dreams under the stars, in silken lace, and with that a moonlight trance, then you are on your way Make midnight whispers, she'll curtsy, and both will dance. To put her onto that pedestal will make a star in a million, this I do promise.

~Love's North Star~
Without warning her love leaves with what he can carry, leaving her behind is what she remembers most. You light is that which knows, [love], the moment when doubt would have her ask, but no surprise on his return she will see he was making room for her. It seems love has a true north within its compass.

~Fears I Tread~
The obstacles in life that challenge us, with 'Much Afraid', the two helpers, 'Sorrow and Suffering', almost instinctive we clear many of the obstacles in life with this constant.

~Fier Battu ~
French for 'Proud Beaten. It speaks of the misunderstood smile which only the 'Mona Lisa' knew about. She remains laconic to this day, as was the day when she posed for Leonardo da Vinci. It is a wry but mysterious smile to say the least.

~A Sense of Feeling Afterwards ~
I have this affinity with John Keats and all that he stands for. This sonnet speaks insightfully as if there was a sense of feeling from the man himself. It is within this letter, one's last words, "And one, 'John Keats'", Romanticism said, to show a sense of feeling afterwards". And so, I did.

~Dancing Forever~

Love takes us on a spin, spiritually, that man makes quite a spectacle of it. But surely, like many of his delusions to put an unknown to the fantasy we see, to change the way we see things when things aren't going our way. Some of us have God's allegiance to innocently bless, alone and without prejudice.

~Wind Chimes~

The title in itself gives a soothing approach while the wooden tubes embellish and unravel the sonnet for us with a chorus known to many that disturbance of a kind diminishing type, the subtle touch I include, like I've said often, a nostalgia from the past to listen to.

~Promised Her till Noon~

I had imagined when alone being with my love, and as I awake with hand outstretched, stretch, to part the curtains. My adoration of the sun pursues nonchalantly. 'Eos', Goddess of the Dawn. Remains, before too long she'd recline from that highest point.

~In Search of the Savi Warbler~

This sonnet can be read backwards with a clue, to compare a warbler sound amid silent verse. Being susceptible to sound I tend to block much of it out. Revealing many of my pet hates as well as rummaging for nought.

~A Pretty Pink Inlaid~

A combination of pink and red roses has been collected to be put in a vase. Thorns have adorned to snag on the skin while arranging them, adding pink combination from them both. The coloured moods themselves present a meek, yet wild cacique behind the dormant scenes.

~Elusive a Song~

A Shakespearean feel on first dates and bucolic scene, and with my lute I would serenade her also. To think of chivalry and the blessed kindness which stirred the clouds among the trees, with frequent notes than I have flung attractive songs hang high among.

~Limelight Beyond the Frieze~

'Fishermen at Sea' was painted by J.M.W. Turner, and a sonnet which explains the dramatic scene. A limelight beyond the frieze shrouded by moonglade glimpses, reflective eaves the depth features, now adding of a generous supply of paint Turner employs, nurturing the sea foam absinth's turquoise.

~En Passant~

3 failed attempts to obtain an annulment from a loveless marriage, and my dealings with the Cannon and a number of priests, who have all since died, it seems my place on the board as the knights. Winning the game means I had won the woman's hand in marriage.

~The Lighthouse Keeper~

A question is asked... "Who is the lighthouse keeper? With the underlying issues outside undermining things, there isn't much a lighthouse keeper can do inside, where warmth has become his isle. It is epic and Biblical in stature to bring God almighty into our very existence to challenge us.

~An Olde World Feel~

This is reading to make you think and learn also, to appreciate the vague and difficult expression was back in medieval times.

~Sicuti Est Natura Rerum~

To honour the man whose first name I have taken, having admired his passion, that Epicureanism is based on the teachings of the greatest good. And that is to seek modest pleasures in order to attain a state of tranquillity, freedom from fear, and to overcome all ills.

~Sword of Damocles~

A great man of power and authority, surrounded by magnificence. In response, Dionysius offered to switch places with Damocles, for one day. Damocles sat on the king's throne, surrounded by every luxury, but to prove a point, a sword would hang above, held by a single hair of a horse's tail, to evoke what it is like to be king, from his enemies.

~De Jure, Puritatem Naturae~

The purity of nature adorns the regret of today's society, given as a warning and spoken by a Puritan from the 16th century, to eradicate such a movement. It speaks of virtue and making good of a bad thing, that the law should remain as it did then than the spectacle it's become. Words are contained in this that have never been heard, up till now.

~Last Words of Past Lives~

A special announcement is attached to the poem, for reasons of misinterpretation, that while we are ready to judge others, it seems the past does catch up with us. That history, would in effect catch up whilst those who are in some way, still pay such a forfeit. Take for instance, the 'Slave Trade'.

~Sprinkling of Harps – Harmonia~

A contest which includes a water colour of a fountain as a subject matter, a weak spray has taken the place of the 'Necklace of Eriphyle', according to Greek legend, [Myth], it would bring great misfortune to all of its wearers, and one so wearer, Harmonia.

~The Ides of March~

It speaks of Ovid in a Classical plague narrative, but only because of Covid, that The Ides of March it denotes, [2020], whereby, between the full moon, 9th March and a supermoon 8th April, the Ides of March would be present. It will combine all dyes and natural taints to delve the fates untimely.

~Now, I Do Not Want to Seem a Hugger Mugger~

The first Women's Rural Institute, 1917, a special guest, a Colonel Richard Stapleton-Cotton, would have been cornered by certain women, but one lucky girl, who slightly embarrassed, [hugger-mugger], to be found alone with him.

~The Final Problem~

Sherlock Holmes increasingly getting close to his nemesis Moriarty, as usual he is aided by Dr Watson. The Final Problem is explained that to have the brain of the first order, then Einstein would have been merely 10 years old when 'Holmes' was pitting his wits with a body language. There are words in this that are not in everyday use.

~Tales of Chivalry~

A 'chatoyant' is a band of bright lustre which shows how transparent chivalry is, an impressionism of a kind, by which the strands are drawn together on matters explained and resolved. That is all importance, prominence, I dare say it must be deemed to rectify not loyalty, but glamour to overall suspicion, with its present-day admiration.

~Lady of the Lake – Excalibur Rising~

Bedivere and Arthur are among the few survivors of the Battle of Camlann. After the battle, at the request of the mortally wounded king. Bedivere casts the sword into the water, at which a hand arises and catches the sword mid-air, then sinks into the waters, and Arthur is thus assured that the sword has been returned.

~Shalott's Love Chants~

An exercise to dispel the lead upto The Lady of Shalott"s downfall, and the discrepancy surorunding a mixture of emotions, hence, her sighs. Her actions are the same as per the orginal, by Alfred Lord Tennyson. It was felt her pent up frustration must not go unnoticed. That her decisions are enacted as well, even before carrying herself in 3D to the boat.

~A Special Devotion~

After 17 years at the world's largest poetry site, one can be spoilt, to find reputable poets who praise you in a way but never overly so. It takes time but eventually you find your way around in as much as you are learning all the same, with different styles.

Thankfully, my writing improved, not least to give praise to those who made a difference when it came to nearing the end of Ray's life. It seems I shall always be indebted for such kindness in a world seemingly at odds with itself with the atrocities we hear, it comforts me to think preferably about the charitable nature of some individuals. I have been in touch with Ray's neighbours, the nurses, and benevolent staff at St Christopher's and of course where Ray had spent his last days, the Villa Maria Care Home in South Croydon.

SPECIAL DEDICATIONS

~1. To My Brother Ray – Bibliographic Record~

In life we must wring out what little success there was in it, to think of Raymond my brother, what little there was I have put into this book. The, 'Bibliographic Record' is one of small mercies and devoted to Ray for the way he went about his life. In fact, to the count he had more friends than I, but that is all down to his warmth and generous heart. There is no way of getting around it that he could have sold sand to the Arabs. It was a gift to being street-wise, and surviving with an honest outlook is credit indeed.

~Parting Through a Shade~

While later on in life we siblings went our own way, but an area near to where we lived, "Long Lane" woods, it was an escape for us kids, to be free from our parents and enjoy the few open space there were around 'The Glade', 'Mardell Road' and 'Longheath Gardens' "A Parting in a Wood" is where we played, it was where we walked on our way to school, it was just one of a few happy memories.

~Significant Weary~

'Whistler's Mother' is a painting I wrote a poem about. After reading the final draught, it very much reminded me of my own mother, who was somehow sadly tortured. It remains unquestionable that she may have ben ill for most of her life. I am sure in her heart, that love remained dormant.

~Sadly, Looking Stone~

For my mother, but on behalf of my father as well, who may have been feeling helpless at the time, or in denial that my mother was hiding something. It most certainly affected our place in and around the neighbourhood as being dysfunctional, our not being friendly.

~Q.E.D. [Quod erat demonstrandum]~

It came out by accident that my mother had had a miscarriage, giving the allowance the effects on a mother have, to early 1950. I would take it to mean my proving what I set out to do. Q.E.D. speaks on a personal note to a 'would be', brother, so proving the same that 'we make a go of it'. Understandably so, since my early childhood and youth was a lonely one.

~Universal Measure~

The 'Universal Measure' as it stands and relentlessly so, that hard work and feeding the family was very much many men's idea of married life. My life revolved around my mother, and my mother's around the moon which in a nut shell speaks of an approximation between woman and woman. The 'housewife' was a general term applied to being house bound and it was expected. In 1969, I would join my father in the foundry doing the very thing my also bringing money into our household, and it wasn't from choice.

~With Posthumous Thanks~

From as far back as I can remember, [1954], until my 10th year, [1961], my favourite grandfather would look after me, and take me on what we call nature walks. I recall visiting his flat in Upper Norwood, which did not confine me to the house. It was more informative and the close bond between us, enabled me to speak rather than be mute as it was looking. Difficulty, mixing with other children was another disclosure.

~Our Courtship – Sonnet Crown~
I would in essence call her, "My first love". Miss Maureen Dunkley came into my life by default. In fact, there were three chance meetings in all, to speak of serendipity. To call it a courtship, it seems time and patience was very much needed for long distance love to work, and for me, lots of 'healing', from a traumatic time 12 years previously. Plus, Maureen had her mum to think of back in India on her own, well, with her dogs to think of. Making it work was above all else being there and being the constant in her life. "Our Courtship – Sonnet Crown", speaks of a fairy tale romance, which it was, and still is.

~Some Healing~
As previously stated, the 'Allpoetry' website became my passion, while away from Maureen. It could be said that poetry is a great healer too. I had taken up long distance running, but it never worked. BUT it was my interacting with like-minded people, the poets who delve on soul relating, it is a beautiful thing to share with others without having them judge you.

~Josephine Vella, Debbie Altiparmakis, Judy Carolyn Roberts, & Rexanne Endicott~
My acquaintance with the said poets, ranges from 7-14 years, that it seems even longer than that, to think of 'Josie', 'Debbie', 'Judy' & Rexanne like sisters, - to Maureen as well. Topics on poetry and hard times it seems we have survived on our merit. What we can share as well is celebrating our, 'getting through good and bad times.' It needn't be complicated; that we all seem to get on well.

~Binding Covenant ~

My praise overall of the NHS, the nurses in hospitals and care homes, the peripatetic idea to save on waiting time, putting the patient first. To see or hear of it first hand has very much changed the way I see helping the sick and frail. The 'Binding Covenant by way one knows what the other is doing, the continuation of care from one to another, it has to be seen to be believed.

I cannot praise enough the people who have cared for us personally. Taking in the fact that 'jokes' and a 'casual' feel would ease the tension around my poor brother at his end, rather than be totally oblivious with nothing to say. There are ways of coping with death and no one can give guidance how to do it. It is beautifully understood that we are given this freedom to grieve and given time to do so. Thanks to the nurses and staff at the Villa Maria Care Home, South Croydon, and St. Christopher's Hospice, Sydenham.

~Quote from Wayne Jents's, "Rise for Titus" ~

The poem from Wayne Jent, "Rise for Titus" came out of the blue during the 'Late Night Poets radio programme. It came as a complete shock. Slowing the tempo for my sake, I didn't even recognise the poem from what I had read, praising me like he had.

~My Learned Trusted Friends

My study of the classics has included many poets, for whom style and panache has brought the occasion to the present day and a similar style. Between Keats and I there is an affinitive

~Virgil~

It is said that nothing is much known about Titus Lucretius, but for his poem, it seems I had read of a love potion he was supposed to have taken, reading from one of my encyclopaedia's. How ironic, my return from India was and my feeling the same way? I felt I should know more about this man. It was after reading, "De Rerum Natura", that I took the name of 'Titus' and some "Enigmatic Verse".

~*Prodigium*~

It seems Virgil was very shy and reserved, just like I. While it is easy to assume that his humble father would have brought a kindly nature out, along with the embarrassment that an education could not be afforded, that poetry would be a credited with diversion. Virgil had abandoned rhetoric, medicine and astronomy for philosophy. By which the route of my own domain took place, poetry, from the Epicureanism school and his close contacts with them would have endeared a further leverage of works from him.

NOTE FROM THE AUTHOR

So untimely was the passing of my brother Raymond, that it coincided with a Full Poetical Works which was nowhere near completion, yet were almost fully installed by the time this sad news came around. These are works which have not been seen by the British public, I thought it best to honour my brother, as a send-off, that such works be included for the book titled, 'Vestige'.

Also, at this critical time, you will find the word 'death', comprised within some of my works. While it is unavoidable to leave this word out altogether, it would be equally damaging, therefore, not to meet it head on to embrace our fears. Those family members who have recently had to deal with such an outcome will appreciate the sentiment.

Beholden are my Affections

Anthony Smith